CURRENT TRENDS
IN
LIBRARY SERVICES

CURRENT TRENDS IN LIBRARY SERVICES

CHERIAN MATHEW

CYBER TECH PUBLICATIONS
4264/3, Ansari Road, Daryaganj, New Delhi-110002 (India)
Ph.: 011-23244078. Fax: 011-23280028
E-Mail: cyberpublicationsdelhi@yahoo.com

CURRENT TRENDS IN LIBRARY SERVICES

First Edition 2011

Published by G.S. Rawat
For Cyber Tech Publications
4264/3, Ansari Road, Daryaganj, New Delhi-110002
Ph.: 011-23244078. Fax: 011-23280028
E-Mail: cyberpublicationsdelhi@yahoo.com

Printed at Asian Offset Printers 9212182454

Contents

Preface

Basically libraries are the repository of knowledge. These are to serve a large number of customers for different needs. Hence libraries have to accomplish various functions satisfactorily under different service systems.

This work is devised to furnish valuable information on various library services. The judiciously selected readings are grouped under the following headings: College Library Services; Library Reference Service; Special Reference Services; Reference Sources; Circulation Services; Women Library Users; Guidelines for Locating Material; Some Legal Issues; Glossary and Bibliography etc.

The information is supported by fact and figures derived from research findings of leading library professionals from all across the world. Definitely, this work will prove vade mecum to all library professionals besides academics, trainers and trainees in the field.

We express our gratefulness to all those men of letters whose works are cited or substantially made use of herein. The real credit this ought go to them all Our teachers, colleagues and friends have rendered yeoman's service by way of guidance, inspiration and assistance. We are deeply indebted to them also. Finally we appreciate our publishers for evincing keen interest in this project and materialising it elegantly in the present shape.

We will welcome suggestions and comments for improving the contents of this which we will incorporate in subsequent edition with due acknowledgement.

—Author

1

College Library Services

> "A thing that you sincerely believe in, cannot be wrong. Because belief does not come at will. It comes only from the Holy Ghost within. Therefore a thing you really believe in cannot be wrong."
>
> —*D.H. Lawrence*

College libraries are the ones having large public to serve. As such every library professional should have sound understanding of the college library services.

In the present chapter we have tried to elucidate college library services. Empirical instances arc cited to support the narration.

It is pertinent to note that primary objective of the college library, is to make its service contribute as effectively as possible to the educational programme of the college. In so doing, it performs certain functions which include:

(1) it provides technical and specialized study materials needed to keep the faculty abreast of their fields;

(2) it provides study and reference materials required for supplementing classroom instruction;

(3) it provides, as far as possible, research materials needed by members of the faculty;

(4) it encourages students to use books independently and attempts to develop in students sound habits of reading;

(5) it participates in such programmes of post-collegiate education for alumni as are sponsored by the college;

(6) it cooperates with other libraries in strengthening the total resources in the region of which the college is a part; and

(7) it provides study materials needed by extension and correspondence students in colleges where such instruction is offered.

Through a clear interpretation of these functions and the activities which are performed in carrying them out—the administration, faculty, students, and others concerned with the welfare of the college should be thoroughly informed as to that the library is and what it does. The success of the college library in carrying out its functions is dependent upon the confidence and respect of those it serves.

Progress can be made only as the record of library achievement is made known. The main objective of library interpretation, therefore, is to assist in making the library an integral and real part of the educational programme of the college.

It follows that if the interpretation efforts are successful in developing confidence in and understanding of the aims and methods of the library, the administration will then see to it that the library receives its full share of financial support.

In fact, library interpretation in most colleges is often a very haphazard affair. This is only natural since a great deal of publicity must of necessity depend on the opportunity to prepare a news article, make a talk, or arrange an exhibit. On the other hand if the results are to serve a useful purpose, there should be a clearly defined programme of interpretation and one person to guide and plan its development. The more systematic and definitely pointed the interpretation plan is, the more effective it will be and more easily managed.

This is not to say that interpretation should be the work of only one person. A simple but effective organization will utilize the skills and co-operation of all members of the staff because above all other persons they are the active agents of interpretation. In the small college library, the librarian will direct the work and plan the organization, largely utilizing student help for carrying out the routines. In the large college library, the work of planning and directing publicity may well be delegated as a part-time activity to a member of the staff working under the direct supervision of the librarian.

It is necessary, of course, for the person to be released sufficiently form other duties to give real attention and time to planning publicity. Such a person would assemble information for local newspaper and student reporters or for the college news bureau, prepare and write the copy for book bulletins, make arrangements with the person in charge of library departments for exhibits and for faculty participation in planning exhibits, arrange for competent student help to make posters and signs and perform other duties related to interpretation work.

Unless some one person gives thought to planning and directing the interpretation work there is real danger that it will become a routine affair, unrelated in any real way to the functions which the library is attempting to perform.

Remarkably, approach to library interpretation is two fold: (1) through personal contact between librarians and the individuals and groups they serve, and (2) through the planned distribution of information about the library. The former is often spoken of as "public relations" and the latter as "publicity", Public relations involves relationships with (1) campus groups: the college administrative officers, boards and advisory committees, the faculty council, department heads, teachers, faculty committees, and students, and (2) off-campus groups the alumni and Friends of the library groups: members of the college community; professional, accrediting, and educational councils and associations, and foundations.

Publicity includes the following media of interpretation: the annual report, handbooks, the college catalogue, book bulletins and booklist, local and student, newspapers, bulletin boards and posters, exhibits and book displays, and the radio. Progressive college libraries are trying to use most of these various types of publicity media. The college catalogue and annual report have always been used though not always recognized as an avenue of interpretation.

College libraries have always had displays and exhibits, but here again these media have often been so routine in nature and hit-or-miss in planing that they have not always proved effective as a means of interpreting the library and making library services more useful to instruction.

On-Campus Library Relationship

Basically, developing an adequate programme of library service is not alone the responsibility of the library. As has been repeatedly pointed out in this book, good library service is a cooperative undertaking requiring the combined effort of the administration, faculty, library staff, and students.

Upon their knowledge of the aims and methods of the library rest their judgement and willingness to cooperate. The relationship of the library to the various campus groups have been discussed in detail in different parts of this book, but it may be well to summarize some of these relationships here in order to show their importance in interpretation. Certain functions in interpretation, such as determining objectives, establishing the proper relationships with administrative authorities, and preparing official reports, are the responsibility of the librarian. On the other hand, the member of the library staff are the persons who come in contact most frequently with the users of the library, and they must have all the facts on policies, methods, and services.

These data are provided partly through staff meetings, bulletins, and booklists but largely through individual conferences between heads of departments and the librarian. It is not enough, however, to have the facts. The attitude of the staff member towards those he helps is even more important. Upon his tact and patience in working with students and upon his competency and friendless in contacts with faculty will depend much of the success of the library and its interpretation programme.

Administrative Officers

Dr. Branscomb points out very clearly that little can be accomplished by the librarian without the support and cooperation of the college president. A majority of librarians are direct responsible to the president. He approves the budget and staff appointments even though the final authority in these matters rests with the board of trustees.

In developing the policies of the library, he is consulted at every step. The librarian's annual report is directed to the president and through the president the major needs of the library are transmitted to the board of trustees. Thus, in most colleges the development of library services is in the last analysis determined by the librarian working closely with the president.

If there are differences of opinion or lack of mutual respect, they must be ironed out or they will inevitably lead to a weakening of library service. It is equally important, states Dr. Branscomb, that the college president should see to it that in the organization of the college "the librarian is not separated from, but rather is brought into vital relationship to, the educational programme." In most colleges this will mean that the president will have to be given a clearer picture of the range and importance of library service in the educational programme than he now possesses.

In a few colleges the librarian is directly responsible to the dean, but in all colleges he has close relationships with the business manager and his assistants. These relationships vary in different colleges but in general involve the placement of library orders, the payment of bills, the checking of library balances, the determination of insurance inventories, the employment of the clerical staff, and the review of the budget.

Satisfactory relationships here are based on common sense and good business administration. The business manager expects the library to be well organized and managed. He will not object to the librarian's taking a strong stand on library needs and support, but he expects him to temper his requests to the known financial ability of the college, to combine the ideal with the practical, and to effect both a balanced library programme and a balanced financial programme.

On the other hand, the librarian has a right to expect full cooperation from the business manager in the arrangements for checking library balances, in safeguarding the library's interests where special funds are involved, in taking a broad educational view and not a penny-saving attitude towards library support, and in assisting the library to meet unusual and unexpected financial obligations which may arise after the approved budget is in operation.

Other important administrative relationships include those with the dean of men and the dean of women in matters of student cooperation and discipline, the personnel officer in the employment of student help, and with other officers in such matters as student counseling.

Administrative Board or Advisory Council

Generally, in most colleges there is an administrative board or advisory council which acts as the planning (executive) committee of the faculty and serves in an advisory capacity to the college president. The board considers matters of affecting the library—such as personnel, finances, and curriculum, policy.

It would seem desirable therefore, that the college librarian should be given a place on the board or advisory council. The library, of all departments on the campus, can least afford to be self-contained. Universities have quite generally recognized the importance of this relationship and have in their statutes or by-laws made provision for the librarian as an *ex-officio* member of the board. But in colleges, the librarian is seldom represented on the board or advisory council.

This is unfortunate since this is one of the important committees on which the librarian might serve, both for his contribution and the increased effectiveness of the library's service which would result. His function on such a board would be to keep library services abreast of new developments and to hold library interests before the group.

The Faculty

Infact, importance of this relationship requires little comment. Without the cooperation of the faculty, the librarian can do little to coordinate library services with instruction. Without adequate to library support, college instruction is handicapped and faculty research is blocked. Library, laboratory, and classroom must be so planned as to reinforce the teaching process in every possible way.

The improvement of library service should therefore be, to a far greater extent than is present the case, a matter of faculty-library cooperation. In most colleges where the librarian is a member of the faculty with professional rank, he is automatically a member of the faculty council and has the right to vote. The faculty council determines the policies and methods concerning admission, teaching, counseling, and examination.

Membership and attendance by the librarian and members of the staff in the council meetings will afford many opportunities for learning at first hand about matters which have an important bearing on library service. Much of the work of the council is done through committees. Where these committees are concerned with educational policy and curriculum changes, it would seem to be the part of wisdom that any administration seeking to improve the conditions of colleges work would se to it that the librarian and the staff members who hold responsible positions are represented on these committees. To relegate the librarians to the status of an administrative assistant or a clerk is equivalent to dwarfing much of the driving force which contributes to the success of a college.

In the highest and best type of library service, the librarian' is more likely to be a liaison instructor between classroom and library rather than a mere clerk handing out books. Although it is unfortunately true that little is done to bring the judgement and experience of the librarian and the members of the library staff to bear on the determination of policies formulated in faculty committees, it is true that the library has other opportunities to establish committees, it is true that the library has other opportunities to establish close relationship with the faculty.

The librarian works closely and intimately with department heads in the preparation of the book budget and in the determination of budget allocations for books. Through the faculty library committee, there is opportunity to discuss and formulate policies which affect jointly the work of the teaching staff and the library.

The staff, in its contact with faculty, furnishes information of first importance in teaching and research. These cooperative relationships are all important in developing a genuinely educational type of library service, and they afford an opportunity to stress the joint responsibility of the library staff and the faculty.

Students

Service to students by the librarians in cooperation with the faculty is the main task of the library. Library relationships with students are conducted mainly throughs:

(1) services at the loan and reference desks and personal conference;

(2) talks, group tours, and instruction in the use of the library and bibliography;

(3) publicity in the form of printed literature, displays, and exhibits, and

(4) the student library committee.

Not more than a half-dozen college have student library committees and few of these are mentioned in the professional writings. Yet close student-library relationships are necessary to an understanding of the conditions of student use of the library and to the development of constructive measures of any sort for improving library service. The student library committee, in the light of its stated functions, may properly be regarded as one device for encouraging friendly associations.

These functions are usually given as follows:

(1) to establish a cooperative spirit between the students and the library staff in order to aid the library in meeting curricular and extra-curricular student library needs;

(2) to encourage students to participate in the recommendation of book purchase for the library;

(3) to help the librarian interpret the objectives, policies, rules and regulations of the library to the student body;

(4) to promote general and recreational reading and to increase student appreciation of good literature;

(5) to forestall criticism of the library by keeping the librarian posted on student library needs, and

(6) to help relate the work of the library to instruction.

Membership on student library committees ranges from five to eight-persons. The committee is commonly appointed by the student government association in consultation with the librarian. Miss Ruby Dare, describing the student committee of the Greenville (III). College library emphasizes the importance of selecting students who have "an interest in literature evidenced by considerable general extra-course reading; a sufficiently attractive personality to be able to lead students; ability to carry responsibility; reliability; and a read enthusiasm for serving on such a committee."

Consideration is sometimes given to class, residence hall, and student library staff representation on the student library committee. The members of the committee ordinarily elect their own chairman. Meetings are usually irregular, with the librarian always in attendance. The duties and work of the student library committees naturally vary according to the special needs of each library. Activities in which such committee have successfully promoted the aims of the library at Rockford, Wellesley, Scripps, Mills, Greenville (III), and Penn. State include the following:

(1) the preparation of book reviews for the student newspaper;

(2) aid in the planning and arrangement of library exhibits in and outside the library building;

(3) assistance in the selection of books of particular interest to student;

(4) planning a programme to encourage students to build their own personal libraries while in college;

(5) supervision of residence hall libraries; and

(6) assistance in making surveys of student opinion and the use of library resources.

Notably, this last activity would seem to be one of great potential usefulness to both students and the library. The library stand to gain understanding, otherwise inaccessible, of conditions of student use of the library, and to benefit in the development of any changes that are made by the sense of general confidence which such cooperation tends to develop. The students gain whatever values may come from friendly associations with the librarians, by the improvements in library service they are able to suggest, and by a broader understanding of the purposes and uses of the library.

The librarian plays an important role in the formation of the committee, in attendance at its meetings, and in guiding its work. In all these activities the remains in the back ground as much as possible. His function is advisory suggesting problems to be considered, discussing possible solutions, and sharing with the committee his special knowledge of library work.

His personality, ability to talk easily with students, sense of humor, and tactfulness and patience in dealing with suggestions and complaints will have to great deal to do with the success of the student advisory committee on the library.

Off Campus Library Relations

The chief values of cooperation between the library and various campus groups have already been suggested. Such relationships are second only in importance to those on campus in a broad view of interpretation because they stimulate personal and professional growth, afford new opportunities for useful educational service, establish contacts which may be helpful in the development and support of the library, and help to interpret the distinctive contribution which college libraries can make to society.

Alumni and to Friends of the Library Groups

Practically, interpretation to alumni may take two forms: (1) lending and reference services, and (2) publicity designed to encourage gifts. The opportunity to provide an educational service to alumni through the distribution of reading lists, the lending of books for scholarly or technical work, and the uses of the reference facilities of the library have already been touched upon in an earlier chapter.

There will be a great diversity in the request received by the college library for information and books loans some of them will be answerable by a book loan or a collection of pamphlet material about a particular subject, others will necessitate a letter in which the specific information is given with reference to sources which may be borrowed by the alumnus from the college library or from some other library.

Still others will lead to conferences between the reference librarian and members of the faculty and will result in the sending of a systematic course of reading to meet the alumnus's particular need. Publicity for gifts may take the form of direct appeals to individual alumni for special purchases or the publication of lists of desiderata in the alumni magazine. As a prelude to either, it is important to build up good relationships by keeping the alumni informed of library progress and development.

In addition to articles in the alumni journal the librarian should take every opportunity to know the alumni and to meet them at reunions. When a person has been out of college for twenty years he has forgotten all about the library. A regular column of library notes in the alumni magazine and an occasional picture of some interesting phase of library work will help to build up interest and goodwill. Some colleges have found that an organization of Friends working steadily and intelligently toward definite goals had added much to the value and usefulness of the library.

In actual practice, these Friends of the library groups are composed largely of alumni. The initiative in suggesting the idea of the Friends organization may well be taken by the librarian. He knows what such organizations have contributed to libraries in other institutions, what has been written about them, and what methods have been used in establishing and keeping them going. Beyond this initial stimulation, the librarian's relationship to the Friends organization is largely a subordinate one.

Unless there is some one person among the alumni or college friends who has the interest, understanding, and energy to take an active part in creating enthusiasm and membership for the organization, the results are not likely to prove lasting or worth while, If the Friends organization is simply the librarian's show and if the group relies on him to keep it going and alive, its value is largely lost. Although the librarian remains in the background in the actual development of the Friends organization, he has an important contribution to makes as an adviser to its promoters and leaders.

At the time of establishment, the Friends organization should be given a "frank and full statement of what the library now is, what it is doing, what it desires to become and how its friends can aid in its progress toward that goal." After the group is established, the librarian is the logical person to furnish the information about gifts that are needed to build up the collections and services.

Unless this relationship exists, there is the possible

danger that the Friends organization may prove an embarrassment to the library by leading to gifts of rare and special collections which are not pertinent to curriculum needs and which result in a heavy administrative expenditure from an already over-taxed budget.

College Community

It is pertinent to note that in both service and interpretation, it is important that the college librarian take into account the community in which the college is located. Some libraries, such as Oberlin, maintain full public library service for residents of the community. In most colleges, provision is made for townspeople to use the library as a reference center and to borrow books of a scholarly or research nature of they are not in use by the faculty and students.

State supported colleges have a great obligation not only to citizens of the local community but to residents of the entire state. Regardless of the nature or extent of library service to the community residents, the library cannot afford to overlook these persons in its interpretation programme. News of the college is published in local newspapers which are often read throughout the state.

Association and Foundations.

Besides the necessity of maintaining close relationships with alumni, friends, citizens of the local community, and the general public, librarians are under professional obligation to participate in the work of their national and state library associations. Moreover, since libraries are an integral part of colleges, librarians are naturally concerned with the interests and activities of educational associations and philanthropic foundations.

These organizations have had a tremendous influence on the whole educational field and have contributed directly to the growth and development of libraries in institutions of higher education It is important, therefore, that college librarians should identify themselves as closely as possible with the aims of these organizations by attendance at some of their meetings, contributions to convention programmes, and by wide reading in their published reports and proceedings.

The value and significance of these outside relationships may be more readily understood by the newcomer to the library profession by review of the purposes and work of the more important of these organizations.

American Library Association. Founded in 1876, the American Library Association is the oldest and largest association in the world. Of its many objectives and accomplishments, three are of particular concern to college librarians:

(1) to raise standards and promulgate ideals of library service;

(2) to assist libraries to operate with the utmost economy and efficiency;

(3) to improve the status of librarians by working to advance salary standards, by maintaining an effective placement and personnel service, and by increasing professional knowledge through original research.

The ALA conducts and disseminates important educational research studies, furnishes comprehensive book selection and bibliographical services, and fosters a programme of sound educational interpretation. The programmes of the Association deal with important current educational problems.

Association of College and Reference Libraries. Of the five major division of the American Library Association, the one most closely identified with college library interests in the Association of College and Reference Libraries. Established as a division under its new name in 1940, though having a continuous existence as a section of the Association since 1889, the A.C.R.L, as it is popularly known, aims "to bring together in an annual meeting college and university librarians and staff members, librarians and staff members of reference libraries, as well as the reference librarians of public libraries, for the discussion of their common problems and the problems peculiar to academic and scholarly work."

Through its section committees journal, *College and research libraries,* it has stimulated experimentation and research for the improvement of college library service and it has helped to integrate the efforts of college, university, and reference librarians with those of kindred groups such as educational and research agencies.

Other National Library Societies. The American Library Association maintains close relationships with six affiliated national societies and nine other national library societies. Although membership is limited to libraries concerned with the collection and service of research materials, librarians in larger colleges are concerned with the work and publications of the Association of Research Libraries. In recent years this Association has made available at a price that most large college libraries can afford a valuable research and catalogue tool in the *Catalogue of books represented by Library of Congress printed cards* (160 vols.) and has continued to sponsor the important annual list of

Doctoral dissertations accepted by American universities. College libraries hold institutional memberships in the Music Library Association and college librarians have contributed to such valuable technical tools as the *Code for cataloging music* and the *Subject headings for the literature of music from the Library of Congress subject headings.* Through its treatment of technical problems in special fields, particularly those relating to the subject and content of college, and university departmental libraries, the Special Libraries Association has furnished valuable aids and tools for the college library.

In the pages of its official bulletin, *Special Libraries.* College librarians are finding practical and useful information on the handling of special collections, audio-visual materials, and ephemeral or fugitive materials. Close relationships exist between college librarians and the Bibliographical Society of America, which has as its purpose the promotion of bibliographical research and publication.

College librarians have served as officers of the Society and as members of its various committees. The semi-annual meetings of the Society have considered bibliographical matters of direct interest of college librarians, such as problem of bibliographical instruction in colleges, The Society has sponsored and published research in which college librarians have participated and benefited,.

State and Local Library Association. State, regional, and local library associations have contributed to college libraries primarily through strengthening the American Library Association and through annual or biennial meetings which have enabled librarians and staff members to come together for informal discussions of common problems.

Moreover, they have challenged, perhaps not so much as they should, college librarians to cultivate a broader view of their profession than is possibly by restricting themselves merely to campus problems. State associations have introduced and interested college librarians in such problems as state aid for public libraries, regional libraries, and reading studies. College librarians, on the other hand, have contributed to public and school members of the state association by discovering and promulgating opportunities for cooperation through the loan of books, the promotion of library exchanges, and the publications and dissemination of bibliographical works and studies, State, regional, and local association sometimes have publicity committees, publish bulletins, and in other ways influence the attitude of the public towards libraries, including those of the colleges.

Accrediting Associations. The work of the North Central Association and the Southern Association of Colleges and Secondary Schools has been particularly beneficial to college librarians. The basis of accreditment as previously indicated is no longer limited to quantitative measurements but is to be found in the adequacy of the book and periodical collection for the academic programme of the particular institution and in the use of these materials by students and faculty. College librarians have played an increasingly active part in the development of the criteria of measurement for the associations.

In 1935, Dr. Douglas Waples and his colleagues at the University of Chicago Graduate Library School developed more exact measures for the evaluation of the part the library plays in the achievement of educational objectives. In June, 1942, the North Central Association again appointed committees, on which college librarians were prominently represented, for revising forms and checklists. In 1940 the Southern Association invited college and university librarians to assist in re-defining its standards for college, teacher college, and junior college libraries; and in 1942 the Southern Association sponsored a work conference on problems of higher education in which the library was a major topic of discussion and in which libraries were invited to participate.

From this brief review, one is perhaps justified in concluding that at no time has the accreditation movement established closer relations with college librarians or shown greater effectiveness in evaluation than it is manifesting right now. More and more, it is plain, accrediting association are taking college librarians into their confidence with reference to the actual evaluation of library service.

The importance of this relationship lies in the increased opportunity it gives librarians to make their services more truly effective in the educational programme.

Learned Societies, Councils, and Educational Associations. College librarians, taking their cue from their university colleagues, are increasingly recognizing the importance of the relationship of the library to learned societies, councils, and educational associations. The councils and associations, on the other hand, are taking a more active interest in recent years than ever before in problems directly and indirectly relate to libraries.

The four major councils are the National Research Council, the Social Science Research Council, the American Council of Learned Societies, and the American Council of Education. Their constituent members include among other associations: the Association of American Colleges, the American Association of Teachers Colleges, and the American Association of Junior Colleges. The constituent associations maintain approved lists of colleges and establish criteria for accrediting which take into account the adequacy of the library.

The four major councils have three major purposes: (1) to be of service to the government; (2) to promote research; and (3) to serve as a coordinating function between the constituent agencies. Unquestionably, the exercise of the last two functions has some bearing on the problems of college libraries. An illustration of this fact is to be seen in the activity of the Social Science Research Council in the promotion of a nationwide movement to collect and preserve source materials in each state.

This activity has been coordinated with the work of various committees of the American Library Association and has resulted, among other things, in the publication of study of the methods and equipment for reproducing research materials by photographic processes.

The importance of educational associations to college libraries lies in the fact that these associations would appear to have comprehended more fully the strategic role of the library in education than many of the administrators and faculty members of individual colleges have. Through the meetings, projects, standards, and publications of these associations, college librarians are finding an increasing opportunity to interpret the educational function of their libraries to college administrators and to faculties.

The Association of American Colleges has frequently stressed the fact that the college library should be coordinated more effectively with the educational and recreational programmes of the college. That point of view was taken in its Library Project of 1937. The purpose of this project was to study the library from the standpoint of the educational effectiveness.

The study was undertaken by Dr. Harvie Branscomb and culminated in the publication of *Teaching with books,* which as the title suggests, has as much to do with the improvement of teaching as with library procedures for coordinating the work of the library with instruction. In 1937 Dr. William Warner Bishop, writing in the bulletin of the Association of American Colleges, pointed out the same general truth, namely, that "success in college teaching in the next few decades will more and more depend upon success in making the college library a true teaching instrument."

In the task of making the library a more vital factor in teaching and in broadening the responsibility for bringing this about, it is apparent that college librarians will bringing this about, it is apparent that college librarians will benefit tremendously by close relationships with learned societies and educational associations.

Hence it behooves college librarians to become acquainted with the purposes of these societies and associations, study their programmes and reports, and establish a friendly basis for cooperative action.

Foundation. The contribution of the endowed foundations to the growth and effectiveness of college library services has been mentioned at several points in this book. It is apparent that these foundations—particularly Carnegie and Rockefeller, and the General Education Board—have played no small part in the development of the college library. The purposes of these foundations in supporting college libraries are similar to those reported above. Summarizing the Carnegie Corporation gifts of over four million dollars for academic libraries.

Foundation money for libraries has gone into buildings and equipment, library, endowments, librarianship endowment, the purchases of books, library surveys, bibliographical research, bibliographical publications, and cooperative projects. In as much as these foundations, more than any other outside agencies, have contributed directly to the support of library service and to the improvement of book collections and facilities, it is of the utmost importance that college librarians be familiar with their policies of philanthropy.

Publicity

These avenues, or media, though which the library may be interpreted vary somewhat in accordance with the size of the college. The large college may use many more; the small college may select certain media and place its emphasis upon these. As the library grows in size and resources, an increasing proportion of its most substantial publicity emanates directly from its own publication—in booklist, bulletins, annual reports, and brochures for special occasions. Broadly speaking, one generally finds that libraries notable for the variety and excellence of their publications are also notable for their administration and service. Regardless of whether this is true or not, however, the librarian as expositor to the good things to be had from the printed page has a definite responsibility to aim at excellence in his own publications. Everything the library issues, from the simplest booklist to the monthly book bulletin, should stand as an example of good work.

Annual Reports

Annual reports such as those most commonly issued—emphasizing the number of new accessions, volumes in the library, and circulation use—are not a positive force in the interpretative programme of the college library. Their effectiveness as a medium of publicity is further restricted because many librarians are preparing reports for too limited a circle of readers. "No longer can the report be regarded as for the eye of the president alone. It is a document that should be read by faculty and governing bodies and by every member of the staff."

Studies dealing with annual reports such as those by Professor Fay in 1934 and Professor Russell in 1936 have been helpful in acquainting librarians not only with present practices, but more particularly with deficiencies in reporting and suggestions for improvement. Professor Russell's questionnaire on college library reports was direct to the librarians of 500 colleges of the liberal arts types. The most significant revelations of his findings were; that fully one-half of the librarians in American colleges either never make a report of any kind or are uninterested in reporting procedures; that there is a tendency for the stronger and better colleges to be more attentive than the weaker colleges to the matter of library reporting; that annual reports are usually not intended for any readers except those directly connected with the college in some official capacity; and that about half the colleges give no publicity whatever to the library report.

Purpose of the Report. There can be no reasonable quarrel with the usefulness of the annual report of the librarian to the college and to the administration. The single necessity of an annual accounting for funds expended in relation to services rendered would be sufficient if no other considerations were involved.

To this purpose, however, must be added others of less obvious but genuinely practical importance:

(1) it serves as a practical device for keeping members of the board of trustees and faculty posted on library purposes and achievements;

(2) the report enables the librarian and the library staff to comprehend the course of events by study of all departmental reports and thereby to discover means for the improvement of service;

(3) it may serve to interest alumni and friends of the library in making donations to meet special library needs;

(4) it is a valuable document for investigation and research in graduate library schools;

(5) it provides a history of the college library and a record of its contribution to instruction; and

(6) it may be considered, in the opinion of Professor Fay, a valuable primary source material for historical and social science classes, when and if the reports of college librarians "progress towards greater unity in form, arrangement, content, and availability."

It is worth noting that, the preparation of the annual report should be an all-year task. A file of clippings and notes will certainly prove useful when it cones to the actual writing of the report, but few librarians have the patience or time to keep such a record. If the library issues a mimeographed booklist of accessions, the notes prepared for the monthly cover sheet will serve as a reminder of outstanding events, salient figures, and important gifts. The successful report is interesting and graphic.

In analyzing the contents of reports submitted in connection with his study, Professor Russell selected twenty-five reports which he considered superior to all the remainder, It would seem probable, therefore, that an analysis of the items treated in these reports would suggests the contents of a satisfactory report. The use of a topical outline, is a help and time-saved in assembling and organizing the material for the annual report. The final form of the report, of course, will vary according to the points which the librarian wishes to emphasize.

Some librarians put a great deal of care and energy into making the report as complete as possible. Others write a brief summary of the chief events and incorporate summary digests of the staff reports. Still others prefer to concentrate on one particular phase of library activity each year and to build the whole report about this topic.

Such a plan has been followed very effectively in recent years by the librarian of Wellesely College. Good writing, careful organization, and individuality are equally essential to all of them however.

Form of the Report. In presenting the information contained in the report a conscious effort should be made to avoid technical expressions and to express the pertinent ideas so that they will be readily grasped by one unfamiliar with library procedures. Graphs and tables are frequently used effectively.

A typewritten copy is the final form in which most college library reports appear, but it is obviously impossible to reproduce sufficient copies economically in this form if the report is to go to a large number of people. Professor

Russell noted in his study that a growing "number of the colleges either mimeograph or print the library report and are thus able to provide enough copies to supply many interested readers." If the annual report is to qualify as a valuable medium of publicity, it should be sent to the president of the college and to other administrative officer, the members of the board of trustees, the faculty library committee the faculty, the library staff, and a select group of alumni, friends, and students.

In addition, an effort should be made to give it wider public notice through a brief summary in the newspapers and alumni magazine. Libraries which issue book bulletins frequently publish the highlights of the librarian's annual report in one issue each year, In some colleges a summary of the librarian's report is published in the president's annual report.

In colleges where this is done, there would still be need for a complete mimeographed or printed report for circulation to the faculty, to library schools, and to friends of the library.

Handbooks

Remarkably, year more and more college libraries are offering their students and faculty some sort of guide to library resources and services. The guides now in print are notable for their variety in scope and their ingenuity in form and presentation. No two publications have quite the same format, content, or tone, since each one naturally reflects the attitudes and needs of a particular institution.

Library Handbook for Students. A library handbook for students may have permanent values. The information its contains may be used by students throughout their undergraduate years as well as after college. "To learn to use the William and Mary College Library," writes the author of the guide of this library, "is (with adaptations) to learn how to use almost any non-technical American library and to provide oneself with one of the most important tools for remaining an educated man or woman". Permanency, therefore, is an advance which handbooks have over certain other forms of printed library publicity. The library handbooks for students is also important for its instructional value and its timeliness. A student writing a paper on Literary culture in colonial Virginia" will need to use the general periodical indexes as well as books. In high school or during Freshman week he has probably heard about the *Readers's guide;* but at the time he had no occasion to use it and has since forgotten that it exists.

A good handbook will explain the general periodical indexes and associate their use with writing themes on current topics. Later, a suggestion from the teacher or the librarian may send the student back to his handbook at the "psychological time". This same quality of timeliness applies to all of the usual types of information found in the handbook—from the discussion of reference books to the schedule of library hours. The library handbook has direct publicity value. In many, if not in most colleges, the handbook is about the only printed matter which the library can afford to publish. If it is well designed and printed, if it is interesting and informative, and if it is distributed at a time when its pertinence to college studies is readily apparent to the student, the handbook not only contributes to the prestige of the library but it also provides a very real link to instruction.

Handbooks are frequently distributed from the various loan desks in the library. Obviously, then there must be something about the cover, the title, or the printing and design on the cover to catch the student's eve. New York University combines a clever cartoon with a good title—*The guide;* Antioch offers the house and lot—*This is your library;* Vassar appeals by the artistic quality of an original print reproduced on the cover; the Woman's College of the University of North Carolina depends on a combination of fine printing, simple design, and a catch title—*Help yourself* A handbook is intended primarily as an instructional leaflet. No amount of "window dressing" will make a good handbook it the text is badly arranged or poorly written. The first thing, therefore, is to maintain the interests kindled by an exciting cover and to present the material in such a way that the student will get the maximum benefit from reading it. It is a marked characteristic of the best library handbooks that they introduce the student to the main services of the library by function or department. To illustrate with one specific example: under the heading, How to find books easily", the Williams College *Library handbook* introduces the card catalog as the logical starting point in investigation, interprets its use by means of sample cards and brief notes, tells what a call slip is and how it should be filled out, directs the student to the stack and the particular section indicated by the call number tells how the book may be charged when found, and repeats briefly the rules and period of loan.

The work "function" is used to describe this method, not simply because it groups material on processes which logically follow one another, but also because it suggests a method of investigation which is an important part of library instruction. The same approach should be used throughout the handbook. An effort should be made to link specific library aids with the student's class problems. The description of periodical indexes offers an opportunity to associate these tools with the preparation of source themes.

The index may also serve as a device for making the association of library aids with class problems more vivid and understandable. The style of the handbook should be simple, friendly, and clear. Illustrations, charts, and diagrams of all sorts are helpful in explaining library aids and guides. A large number of the smaller college libraries, and a few of the larger, mimeograph their handbooks. A printed handbook is superior to any reproduced by the newer printing substitutes, and it need cost very little more if careful attention is paid to the method of printing and revision. From the angle of economy, such items as library hours, library staff, and rules may be printed on the inside of the cover, front and back, because these are the items most frequently revised.

Library Handbook for Faculty. The preparation of a college library, handbook is made difficult by the necessity for keeping in mind a variety of readers—the tyro and the sure-footed, the indifferent students and the serious student, the bewildered freshman and the experienced faculty member. Most libraries attempt to strike a happy medium, and to present the essential information for all types of readers in single handbook. A few libraries have given considerable thought to this problem and attempt to meet the needs of different readers by separate handbooks or by a special arrangement of material. Pennsylvania State College and the Woman's College of the University of North Carolina issue two handbooks, one for undergraduates and one for graduate students and faculty members. Some duplication of the material in the student library handbook is inevitable but there are distinct advantages to having two handbooks. A hand-book for the faculty serves two purposes.

It is an administrative device for keeping the faculty

informed of library methods, staff personnel, hours of service, and like details. As such, it serves a useful reference purpose. In the second place, it promotes library faculty cooperation and library effectiveness in teaching. This second and more important purposes is not accomplished unless the handbook contains information on such matters as these; a clear statement of book policy defining faculty responsibility as participants in book selection; the necessity for some organization within the teaching department to insure systematic checking and ordering of library materials; the special collections and special materials (films, records, etc.) available in the library for supplementing modern methods of teaching; the policy of the library in regard to helping students with reference services; the responsibility of the faculty in making assignments to library material; and the facilities of the library for the promotion of research.

Frequent revision is perhaps not as essential as in a student handbook, but a thorough indexing greatly facilitates its use.

College Catalog

The college catalog is sent to all prospective students applying for admission to a particular college and to other institutions of higher learning. This would seem to stamp it as an important medium for interpreting library services, but actually it has not been used for this purpose by librarians except to record the more obvious facts of size and to inform students about hours, regulations, and directions for finding materials in particular departments or rooms in the library.

Specific deficiencies noted by Miss Florence King in her extensive study of the library in the college catalog included the following:

1. The library is given a relatively small space in the college catalog in proportion to the importance of its instructional function.
2. The catalog is indexed inadequately for the purpose of making available all information about the library and library personnel.
3. In respect to matters of administration, organization, and service to readers, the library does not receive the attention it deserves in order to present sufficient, significant, and effective information for either the student or the professional group.
4. The importance of the library is obscured in the catalog by the unfortunate position of descriptive information which tends to emphasize its architectural rather than its instructional character.

In fact, a consideration of the purposes of the college catalog will help to show its value as a medium of interpretation for the college library. In the first place, it is intended to acquaint prospective students and their parents with an accurate statement of what the college offers in the way of a sound education. Therefore, it should include a statement of the place of the library in the college programme and of its book and periodical resources for serving instruction.

Direct teaching services such as library talks and group tours during Freshman week, instruction in the use of the library, and printed handbooks and guides should be mentioned. The assistance given to students at the reference and readers' advisory desks should be stressed. Special materials of value to teaching—such as slides, pictures, maps, and pamphlets—should also be mentioned. Since the catalog is intended primarily for student reading, the description of library resources and services should be direct and simple in language.

As a reference tool on the campus, the catalog is in constant use by teacher and students. It should contain a brief summary of library rules and regulations and specify the hours of library service during the regular session, summer session, and vacation periods. All important information pertaining to the library should be fully indexed, particularly when this information appears in two or three different places in the catalog.

Library facilities close by and available to faculty and students should be mentioned in terms of their special usefulness to these groups. The library staff should be listed as a group and those with academic ranking should also be listed in their proper place with the teaching faculty. Another group to whom the catalog represents the college is the prospective donor. Full descriptive and qualitative information should be given about special collections. As a general rule little is said about these special collections beyond a mention of their names and those of the donors who are responsible for them.

A brief description of their contents not only implies a proper recognition of the importance of special collections but increases their usefulness to research workers. The knowledge that a library has such collections, takes proper care of them and relates their use to instruction may prove an incentive to other benefactors to make donations to the library. The catalog is an important source of college history. Without detracting from the main purpose of emphasizing the relation of the library to instruction, it should be possible to set forth briefly the important highlights of college library history in the catalog and to add, from year to year, significant which will be of special interest to the future historian.

The Newspaper

Newspaper publicity is valuable in a college library for three principal reasons; it enables the library

(1) to explain its resources and services to students and to faculty;

(2) to interpret its broader functions to the public at large; and

(3) it enhances the opportunity of the library to win public support for additional endowment from private sources or for increased appropriations form the state legislature.

The first objective is realized mainly through articles in the student newspaper and the last two through articles in the local, state, and national papers.

Student Newspaper. The student newspaper provides an outlet for library interpretation through news articles, feature stories, book columns and student editorials. The aim is to make the students aware of the value of the library in their education and to stimulate them to use its resources. News articles are best handled through interviews with students reporters. If the librarian makes arrangements for a regular interviewing period at the beginning of the year, it will improve the chances of having a continuous appearance of library news in the student newspaper.

The following types of stories have appeared frequently as news stories in student papers; remodelling and other physical changes in the library building, staff activities (personnel changes, staff member appearing on radio programme, etc.), rare book exhibits book displays in special fields, new rules and regulations, student library prize awards recent accession to the magazines, important magazine articles of the month, recent books, browsing room talks and music concerts, special collections, gifts, and special facilities for student study. Obviously the list is almost limitless and could be extended in each college, depending on the current happenings and the resources of the library. Feature stories which interpret library services or special resources are even more important than news stories. In every college library there are pamphlet collections, bibliographical tools, government documents, and special services which are not used so much as they should be because students do not known about them or do not understand their usefulness.

Articles about these materials or service are more likely to be accepted as feature stories for the student newspaper than for the city newspapers, particularly if a member of the library staff prepares the material and "puts into the story an interest that the editor might have neither time nor inclination to find."

Feature stories have appeared in student newspapers on the resources and services of the library as a whole, on special collections in the library, on the kind of questions received and answered to the reference desk, on the card catalog and special catalog and indexes, and on student reading interests as shown through the circulation records. The same kind of interpretation is made possible through a regular library column in the student newspaper, although the emphasis in the column is usually on new books or books about a particular subject. Student editorials about the library have pointed to the need for additional space, to student honor in borrowing and in handling library books, and to the educational opportunities to be found in using the library.

Local Newspapers. Events in the college library which possess news possibilities to local and state papers are rather limited unless the library receives numerous gifts and possesses collections of unique or special regional interest. If the college is large enough to have a separate news bureau division, the library news should be prepared in rough form for the person in charge of this office.

If this person is made to realize the aims and objectives of the library, and if he is given an insight into the nature and importance of library materials and services, he will probably do his best to see that library news in presented even though it may not have the "spot news" value of the "Betty Coed" Type of story. If the publicity releases originate with the library, such as in colleges where there is no news bureau or person designated to send out college news, certain techniques of modern news-writing must be complied with before the articles are to be considered for publication.

These principles are summarized by Miss Marie D. Loizeaux in her *Publicity Primer* :

1. Place the name of the library in the upper left hand corner of page one, together with the name of the person sending the story, position, release date.
2. Copy should start one third or halfway down the first page; do not caption or title a story.
3. Number all pages after the first.
4. There should be no hyphenation at the end of lines and no dividing of paragraphs from one page to another.

5. The first paragraph must answer the questions, who? when? where? why? and what?
6. The copy should be written with accuracy, brevity, and clearness.
7. The word "more" should be written on the bottom of the page to indicate that copy is unfinished and is to be continued on the next page.
8. The end of the story should be indicted by an "end mark".

Besides the techniques involved, the story itself is the chief concern of the news editor. Miss Loizeaux stresses the importance of "making the story interesting" and of "writing with the non-user of the library in mind." College library stories—at least those which are significant from the point of view of library interpretation—are rarely of the light, human-interest type. Their chances of being accepted for printing are determined in large part by their significance and the appeal of the lead, or opening sentence in the first paragraph. With the increasing emphasis placed on news photographs, it is probable that the library story would receive more favourable attention on the part of the newspaper editors if it were accompanied by photographs. The point is usually made that pictures should feature people rather than objects and that close-ups of a reader using library tools is better than a large group picture.

Bulletin Boards and Posters

Primarily, Bulletin boards and posters offer many possibilities for interpreting library services. They may be used to stimulate interest in selected books on a particular subject; to call attention to special resources and services; to present short, graphic summaries of important national and local news; and to announce programmes and lectures. Posters not only guide and instruct but have cultural values also.

A striking poster may satisfy a student's aesthetic instinct as completely as a beautiful piece of sculpture or a finely printed book. In planning bulletin boards, it has been found useful to keep an informal file of ideas for bulletin board use—titles that appeal, slogans, notes on special days, authors, and events, pictures, book jackets, and pictorial or outline maps. An effort is made to tie national, educational, literary, scientific, and seasonal events with the use of library materials.

Local news clippings are most important—radio programmes, newspapers and magazine clipping about persons and things of local interest, etc. The lesser-known materials which form the background of reference service are often emphasized, such as pamphlets, government documents, bibliographies, and special collections. Attentions is called to services as well as to materials.

All too often students and faculty are not aware of the help they can get through the reference and readers' advisory services of the library. Bulletin board displays will not command attention unless some care is given to their arrangement and design. An experienced librarian publicist emphasizes these details in bulletin board arrangement :

1. Few displays should be shown simultaneously in one room.
2. Neatness, simplicity and visibility are essential.
3. Captions and slogans should be brief and arresting, unhackneyed, confined to a single idea, yet expressed with clearness and force.

4. When the subject is changed, the form of the display should be changed, or else the color scheme, or both.
5. Pictures, jackets, captions—all should emphasize on idea.
6. Long lists of explanations on the board will not be read.
7. A few book jackets, neatly trimmed, and well displayed, are more effective than a great many shown at one time.
8. Illustration should excite interest and be to the point, be large enough to be visible at a distance, simple in design, and with no unnecessary detail.
9. Background materials may contribute color, but should be less intense than the rest of the display; can be varied, but must be planned to harmonize with the materials exhibited and the room in which used.
10. Long lists of explanations on the board will not be read.

The poster collection may be supplemented by clippings from magazines and by purchase or gift from educational and commercial firms which make and distribute posters. *Leads No. 7,* from the American Library Association, gives specific sources for posters and display materials. The sources of maps listed therein may be supplemented by the excellent bibliography of pictorial maps compiled by Miss Betty Brown. Educational and library posters may be obtained from the National Association of Book Publishers, Metropolitan Life Insurance, Co., National Child Welfare Association, National Safety Council, the H. W.

Wilson Co., and other associations and publishers. Most of the home furnishing and picture magazines contain excellent poster material is their cover, text, and advertising pages. Textbooks from the fields of visual education contain sources of posters and charts. Certain colleges publish lists of posters of particular interest for display in connection with subject materials. Display material sources are listed in articles and pamphlets and in practically every issue of the library journals.

Book Bulletins and Booklists

College library publications of this type may be divided into four groups according to their format, contents, and purpose:

(1) book bulletins,

(2) mimeographed list of new accession,

(3) book-lists and

(4) Friends of the library bulletins,

Book Bulletins. Printed periodical book bulletins in college libraries are rare. The reason, of course, is obvious. A successful bulletins is expensive and takes times to edit. A monthly of any size and distinction will scarcely cost less than five hundred dollars a year, and two of the best quarterlies now published cost, on an average, seventy-five dollars an issue for publication costs alone. In terms of hardheaded investments, it is unlikely that the library will receive in the early years of bulletin publication an equivalent in cash or book gifts. Library bulletins are primarily a means for increasing the usefulness of a library.

Only indirectly may they help to build up goodwill and support. It is not uncommon, for example, for the editor of a book bulletin to mention special books which the library cannot afford to purchase from its regular budget. And not infrequently one reads in a later issue the acknowledgment of a gift of some of these items form a reader and friend of the library. The library bulletin increases the usefulness of the library by calling attention to new books received by the library and by interpreting library services to students and faculty and alumni. The library way of doing things and its resources are frequently unknown and a little mysterious to many of its readers. The book bulletin offers an opportunity to clear up these mysteries; to explain the work of the catalog the order, and the circulation departments; to label and interpret such intangible services as personal guidance in reading and using the library; to describe exhibits and special collections and to call attention to materials and services which are of little use because nobody knows about them.

Although it is not widely removed from the current pattern of printed bulletins, Dartmouth's *Library bulletin* has assets which make it a worthy model for study. It came out first in 1931 and has been the inspiration of many other bulletins since then. Its appearance is pleasing and it never fails to make the most commonplace incidents in library work interesting and amusing. Distinction and beauty are contributed through the choice of a rich quality of paper and fine typography. In the main, however, its excellence stems directly from the variety, interest, and graceful literary style of its contents. This is accomplished in two ways. First, in approaching every aspect of the work of the library—from rare books down to the most mechanical operation in library routine—the editor of the bulletin thinks primarily in terms of his readers. Second, the style of writing is direct,, pleasant, and witty.

There is nothing official or impersonal about it, some

of the types of material qualifying for admission to its pages include:

1. Special collections
   - Americana
   - Italian dialect collection
   - Nineteenth- and twentieth-century Spanish plays
   - Art library
   - Medical library
   - Map collection
   - Music resources
   - Pamphlet collection
2. Explanation of library policies and rules
   - Open-stack policy
   - Reclassification problems
   - Faculty return of books
   - Book selection
   - Files
3. Publicity and interpretation
   - Notice of exhibits
   - Excerpts form the librarians's annual reports
   - Lists of desiderata
   - Acknowledgment of gifts
   - Notable purchases of indicating liens of interest
   - Friends of the library
4. The work of department
   - Interesting summaries of the

functions and procedures in
Catalog department
Order department
Periodical,
Reserves
Bindery
Treasure room
Tower room (recreational reading)

5. Special services
   - Inter-library loan
   - Photostats and film
   - Research services
6. Booklists
   - Recent accessions—selected and briefly annotated
   - Occasional articles about books on a special subject
   - New periodicals
7. Archival material
   - Reprints of interesting and often humorous letters and documents from the college archives
8. Fillers
   - Amusing incidents relating to service
   - Bookish notes

Special emphasis is placed on the format of the book bulletin to the end that it will not only appear attractive to the reader but also reflect credit on the library whose name it bears. Three college library book bulletins add variety by using a different-color paper stock for the covers of successive issues. Their type is large enough for comfortable reading and in proportion to the size of the page, A six by nine inch page appears to be a favourite size, and six of the book bulletins run to about twelve pages a copy, Local printing costs, the size of the bulletin, the use of illustrations, and the quality of the paper stock influence publishing expenses. Therefore it is impossible to estimate accurately the cost of a "typical" bulletin.

Mimeographed Lists of Recent Accessions, Mimeographed book lists for out number all other forms of library publications for general distribution. Some of the best of these have qualities in common with the book bulletins just described, although their main purpose is to record the new acquisitions. The actual publication cost is small. In planning a mimeographed booklist to keep the faculty informed of new additions the librarian can take the entire stock of current additions for material or he can make a selection. In the large college library it may not be either desirable or justifiable to issue a complete serial list of current accessions, but since the demand for this information comes from the faculty who want to know what books are being added in their own and related fields, it would seem desirable to aim at completeness whenever possible.

If selection is essential because of bulk of current accessions, then it is better to eliminate certain classes of material which are less likely to be of use to the larger group than to attempt a haphazard selection of titles from the accessions of each month. One library omits foreign language, fiction, juvenile and professional library books from its listing. The format and arrangement of the mimeographed lists of accessions are as varied as their titles, Most libraries follow the classification scheme of their libraries, giving suitable captions for each class and arranging titles alphabetically under class. Another plan is to classify the books by subject and to arrange the subjects alphabetically throughout the list.

In most cases the information for each title consists of the call number, author, title and date of publication. For the mimeographed list of accession, as for the book bulletin, a distinctive title is of considerable importance. Some titles used for the lists include: *Stray library leaves, On the shelf, Library book list, Library leaves, Scout, New books, Recent accession,* and *Monthly record.* Variety and appearance are enhanced by changing the colour of the cover sheet in consecutive issues and by using to printed masthead for the title on the cover sheet. While the demand for the mimeographed list of current accessions comes mainly from the faculty, the thing that keeps the publication alive is the librarian's ambition to have a regular channel of communication with the faculty. Few librarians overlook the opportunity to use the introductory pages of each number for presenting interesting and informative notes about staff activities, exhibits, gifts, and new services.

> Items which qualify for admission to the introductory page of the mimeographed list of one library include the following:
>
> Statement of policy concerning the loan of bound periodicals, stack use, etc.
>
> New periodicals and continuations
>
> Annotated list of important additions to the reference collection
>
> Gifts and acknowledgments of gifts

Faculty publications of the month

Descriptions of important exhibits

Circulation statistics interpreted

Notes on little-known sources of information in the college library

Notes on instruction in the use of the library.

Booklists. In addition to book bulletins and mimeographed lists of accessions, some libraries print or mimeograph booklists. Most libraries are either too small, or insufficiently wedded to print, to make the former a practicable proposition. Fewer still are the college libraries that have reported their experience with booklists. For purposes of illustration one has to turn to the university library field. For a number of years now the University of Washington library has been experimenting with booklists in an effort to stimulate student reading beyond their class assignments. Subjects are chosen with the interests of students uppermost in mind; *Poetry Learning to listen,* and *Your private library.* Current discussion prompted. *Consumer help thyself* and *Why democracy?* Purely literary interest suggested; *Some foreign novels in translation* and *Historical novels.* Many were prepared in response to faculty and student requests; *Elizabethan scene, Americas to the South, Map of America,* and *Canada. All* books are ready by the compiler of the list and the book notes are original. A distinctive feature of the lists are the illustrated covers.

They are designed by staff members or students artists, For the most part they are original, although a few are adapted from pictures or are copies. The lists are printed on a sheet four by eight inches and the illustration appears on the front cover. This size is convenient for display and for mailing. Approximately eight to ten lists have been issued annually. The expense of publication is kept low by reproducing the illustrations and text by the lithograph process. Booklists can be mimeographed or typewritten if only a few copies are needed for posing on library bulletins boards, Titles should be listed with sufficient bibliographical detail to enable the reader to secure the book quickly form the stacks or shelves and should be accompanied by brief, readable annotations. Copies are distributed through book displays in the library, by professor in classes, at the loan desks, and the through the mail to selected libraries and to individuals who request them.

Friends of the library bulletins. The final group of library publications to be mentioned at this point is the Friends of the library bulletins. There are may of these published on behalf of university libraries, few in the interest of college libraries. Several of the library book bulletins, previously mentioned, are distributed to Friends regardless of whether the Friends organization contributes directly to the sponsorship of the bulletin. The necessity for a separate Friends bulletin will depend largely on the interest and generosity of the Friends. In place of a periodical publication, some college libraries issue an occasional brochure commemorating gifts of Friends or calling attention to needs whether or not there is any formal organization of a group or association by that name.

Book Displays and Exhibits

Book displays are generally intended to call attention to books for immediate circulation, to encourage browsing, and to help the reader in his selection of books. Exhibits have a more specific aim. They are intended to tell a logical story. The book, pamphlets, objects, or other materials used in the exhibit are not available for immediate circulation. The exhibit "must be preserved as a *whole* during the period of the exhibition." A single theme must be stressed throughout so that the student comes away with a tangible idea, easily remembered. Whether the book display consists of one book or a group of books, it should catch the eye and stand out from the surrounding objects in the room. The various parts of the display, such as the poster or book legend, should help to carry out the idea of the display.

Color, compelling slogans and skillful arrangements of the books have a great deal to do with the way in which a displays is able to circulate books. The practice of placing several books displays in various parts of the library where many readers pass or come to study is important. A single book placed on a stand in a prominent place on the loan desk will often circulate immediately if a brief note or caption suggests it timeliness and particular interest. Many college librarians have found it worth while to prepare subject displays for use outside the library in college buildings where institutes or some special programmes are being held. Independent reading is encouraged by providing a continuous flow of new books attractively and invitingly arranged to catch the student's eye. One library has its *Under the clock* collection of popular titles; another its *Week-end shelf* which is filled with selections from the new acquisitions. These display centers may well become routine in order that students will from the habit of selecting a book for leisure reading. Some college libraries give their students an opportunity to see all the new books. They put all their new acquisitions on display for a week where students and faculty may look them over and leave reservations for those books they would like to read. This plan has the advantage of letting students see all the new books an opportunity they would not have if the books were sent directly to the faculty members who ordered them. It is the function of education to lead students to discriminate between the better and the worse, to arrive at a higher standard. Book displays can contribute to this aim by calling attention to older standards works, primary sources and the more important monthlies and quarterlies which students all too frequently neglect for the digest magazine or the pictorial weekly. If the book display is built around a *subject,* readers are less likely to be concerned whether the books are new or old. Little-known but useful books form the Reference room collection should be brought out and displayed. The success of public libraries in luring readers from the novel or play to history and science through movie tie-ups should not be overlooked by the college librarian. Most book displays will naturally be developed in connection with the student's class work, but supplementary suggestions may be secured from reading lists, library book bulletins, and library annual reports.

Librarians gave first place to exhibits about particular countries and localities. Such exhibits aimed to cover the history, culture, geography, social life, and customs of the countries represented and two-thirds of the exhibits dealt with North American countries. Other subjects, listed in descending order of frequency in the Reagan study, included the following : current events, graphic arts, literary and author anniversary exhibits, book arts, college history, special types of materials such as rare books and little-known resources of the library, and collective and individual biography. Most of the following types of exhibits were reported less frequently but were found in more than one college: exhibits on the Negro, religion, drama, Greek and Latin classics, holidays, science vocations, arts and crafts, photography, architecture, education, geography, home economics, Indians, music, and physical education. In general, Miss Reagan found very little evidence of a systematic effort to make exhibits an integral part of college courses. When exhibits were related to academic subjects, they were restricted to one or two subject fields and were systematically promoted in only two or three libraries. While there is little doubt that most college libraries could improve the educational importance of their exhibits by attempting to relate them to curricular purposes, it should not be overlooked that there are strong practical objections to such a plan.

In the first place there are other opportunities in the library programme where it is perhaps more important to seek faculty cooperation than in the preparation of exhibits.

In the second place it is practically impossible to get around to all departments in such a programme. As a result, the relating of exhibits to the course of a few teaching departments is likely to exaggerate the importance of those particular courses which lend themselves to visual display, and correspondingly to diminish, interest in others which may be of equal importance in a student's education.

There is also the factor of self-advertisement, seized upon by certain teachers who are always on the alert to any means of making their work stand out. Finally, the primary objective of exhibits should be to stimulate the student mind to broad social and cultural interests. Education is not confined to courses but extends to every phase of student life. Exhibits should emphasize the obvious fact that there are more ways of becoming educated than by merely taking courses. Exhibits should stimulate student initiative, breadth of view, and intellectual curiosity. The evidence revealed in Miss Reagan's study shows that for the most part the better college libraries are planning exhibits which are accomplishing these very purposes.

Radio

Little significance is attached by most college librarians to the possibility of relating the radio to college objectives and library interpretation Few librarians participate in radio broadcasts although many college faculties put on radio programmes of some sort. Those college librarians who are concerned with the possible uses of radio in library work have two main approaches:

(1) providing radio programme guides and supplementary reading services, and

(2) participation in radio broadcasts.

For the library to experiment in either direction requires the part time of a member of the staff who has faith in the value of project, enthusiasm for its advancement and development, and some knowledge of recent scientific studies of the effects of radio on reading.

Programme Guides and Services. As a basis for determining procedures in developing broadcast guides and supplementary reading services, a study was made of the listening habits of approximately one hundred students in a particular college.

On the basis of this study and from information obtained from other colleges, it would appear that libraries might usefully render these kinds of radio service to student and faculty listeners:

1. Serious talks, though not as popular as music, news, and drama, have a relatively high ranking for their value

to students in college courses and have a considerable reading "pull." Therefore, they need to be more publicized. They appear at more irregular times on the air than certain music programmes in which students show most interest, and they are more apt to be overlooked unless attention is called to them. In its simplest form this entails setting aside prominent bulletin board space in the library for posting advance notices of programmes. Eye-arresting captions on bright-colored poster paper should call attention to the announcements. It also means selecting programmes for the bulletin board from the various bulletins and announcements of broadcasting companies.

2. On national radio programmes there are symphonic and opera programmes, news reports, talks, and book programmes which lead to a certain amount of follow-up reading. Students reported having followed-up such radio programmes with library reading in current news journals, popular science journals, specific plays and books mentioned in the broadcast, stories of operas, composers' lives music appreciation books, and librettos. Interest in opera broadcasts may be encouraged by prominently located bulletin board displays of pictures of operatic stars; synopses of operas to be broadcast and librettos should be available for use in listening to the programmes. Books, pamphlets, and librettos may be displayed in a case beneath the radio bulletin board and tied up with the programme announcement above.

A great deal of reading matter directly pertinent to the programmes may be obtained free from programme sponsors or the broadcasting companies. Reprints of important lectures and talks are often available free of charge or for a very small cost. These should be displayed, singly or in quantity, along with such books and journal articles as are put on display.

3. The college radio programme will provide similar programmes to encourage study as well as reading, programmes such as music appreciation lectures and music broadcasts, interpretation of events back of the news, travel talks, adaptations from great dramas, poetry readings, and popular knowledge talks. The library has a special responsibility to call attention to these programmes and most departments will readily cooperate in supplying photographs of speakers, programmes announcements, and even copies of scripts. There is opportunity here also for aid to faculty broadcasters and script writers. Several libraries report that they furnish information for members of the faculty and the student body for talks on the college programme series.

4. Several colleges report library tie-ups with student-faculty listening groups, particularly in connection with radio programmes designed to stimulate discussion and debate. A very good example of this sort of cooperation was reported in print by the Syracuse School of Citizenship Library in connection with the *Town Meeting of the Air* Broadcasts.

Participation in Radio Broadcasting. Direct participation in the radio broadcast on a scale to amount to anything has been confined largely to state college libraries. The library of Iowa State College, for example, has worked closely with the extension staff of the college in using the radio to encourage reading and to promote the extension to library facilities throughout the state. In 1938 the librarian in charge on extension service reported: "Now the library time on the air has increased so that one full time person is employed for broadcasting under the supervision of the librarian with several assistants spending part time on radio work. The college library is now on the air twelve times a week, the periods varying from five to thirty minutes. The programmes include book reviews, travel, public affairs, short stories...and a book which is read serially six days a week."

2

Library Reference Service

> "Not all educated men are college graduates, nor are all college graduates educated men. An educated man is one who is useful to humanity, his profession or trade, and to himself."

It is pertinent to note that reference service is insparable, and inherent part of libraries.

In this chapter we shall deal with reference service in detail. First we will take economics of library reference service which will be followed by reference practice.

As mentioned above reference service seems an inevitable part of libraries, Inseparable, Inherent. It was there when we visited our first public library. It accompanied our struggles through college. It was part and parcel of our days in library school. As for many an "institution," familiarity may have led the library profession to take it for granted, assume its benefits and unquestioningly accept its costs.

For some practitioners of the reference art, interest in the "dismal science" of economics and reference service intersect only at the point of arguments for increases to the reference budget. But, of course, this isn't the whole story. It's not even accurate as far as it goes.

Libraries have always been and remain, extremely expensive. This may seem counter–intuitive to readers fresh repairs to dilapidated equipment, expert at conjuring a few dollars to purchase just one more book, bloody from slashing serials subscriptions, or lusting hopelessly after the newest computer or communications technology. From the inside our libraries and media centers seem anything but "high priced," especially in view of the benefits we provide.

But, from the perspective of our parent institutions and taxpayers we appear decidedly "high–maintenance." For example, in fiscal year 1992–93 alone it cost just under $8 million to operate ONE of the nation's smallest, least opulent research libraries (The University of Alabama). In 1991, the total operating income of public libraries in the United States was $4,654,000,000. And in academic year 1984–85. operating expenditures for U.S. public school libraries and media centers totaled $1,182,280,000. And to make matters worse, the quantity of information proliferates even as the lure of costly, new media combines with inflationary pressures to push each of our libraries further behind. Each of us is all too well aware that resources have failed to keep pace.

Communities find it more and more difficult to support public libraries adequately in the face of competing, often critical needs. The boom years enjoyed by academic and research libraries are of the past–a temporary anomaly not expected to recur. With needs expanding and becoming more expensive while increases in resources stall, libraries of all types and in all regions face a gravely challenging future.

Warren Haas has observed that " . . .coping with growth has, in a very few years, been replaced by a need to make fundamental changes in the very definition of what a library is and to recast operations and services in a dramatically different mold . . .under real economic restraints."

From Washington to Main Street tax-payers and consumers continue to demand greater accountability from public agencies and, especially, education. Legislatures and governing boards must respond. In recent years, regional accrediting agencies have adopted new standards requiring colleges and universities to assess and evaluate programmes to verify achievement of educational out comes.

As long ago as 1979 Drake and Olsen recognized for academic libraries that:

> Changing economic conditions and pressure for greater productivity from the public sector will be the major factor stimulating innovation in libraries. It is clear that institutions of higher education can no longer afford traditional libraries and comprehensive collections. Increasing wage rates and changes in consumer demand will force reallocation of library resources to provide funds for capital investment, more efficient operations and more responsive services.

Cummings extended this theme with the warning that "Tolerance for the view that libraries are intrinsically valuable is changing as a result of financial constraints . . .," and that " . . . the need to justify the high costs of libraries requires that some effort be made to measure costs, benefits and cost–effectiveness of various important function."

Reference services, although their costs are frequently buried in library–wide aggregates for personnel, materials acquisitions, etc., are very "high–maintenance." In a 1983 report on the application of econometric models to the costs associated with units within college and university libraries, Kantor found that the median cost of a ". . .reference query dealt with . . ." was $14.00, and that reference functions consumed 20 percent of total budgets. Simplistically and, no doubt inaccurately, applying that percentage to the 1992–93 expenditures of the small research library alluded to above indicates that reference services cost some $1,600,000.

To the extent the Cummings is correct in concluding that our several constituencies no longer find libraries "intrinsically valuable" and that expense must be justified by benefits, reference librarians will be well–served by familiarity with the tools of the economist. As Kantor suggests, reference service is expensive and represents a substantial portion of libraries' expenditures. At the same time, the effectiveness of that service appears less than self-evident.

Basic Concepts

Others sources provide clearer, more authoritative introductions to the economist's artistry than this author should attempt. But, a shared understanding of two fundamental principles is necessary to our discussion. Library budgets, at least in any given fiscal year, can be thought of as modified "zero–sum games," exchanges where " . . .the sum of the winnings is always zero, with one player winning what the other loses." If we think of the various library activities, units, or functions as "players," then the library's budget becomes a "game" with "winning" and "losing" measured in dollars. Assuming no overall budget increase (an all too familiar situation), if support of reference service is to increase, then the portion of the budget and the real dollars, going to one, several, or all other areas and functions must decrease by an equal amount.

A "zero–sum game." An additional reference librarian will result in that amount of salary and benefits not being available to pay for a cataloger, student assistants, travel expenses, books, or serials.

A subscription to a new machine–readable index will result in the funds equalling the cost of that subscription (i.e., license fee, equipment, maintenance) not being available to pay for subscriptions to periodicals indexed by the new index and not available for on–demand purchase of individual articles from a commercial vendor, or any other purpose. Even if the budget increases, "zero–sum" logic applies. With enough budget increase, the addition of a reference librarian or index subscription will not require an actual decrease in funds for other areas in the library. Nevertheless, any increase (proportion of the budget) that reference receives denies other areas or functions that specific potential increase, thus diminishing the potential for increased output in those areas.

Another important and useful concept, closely related to the "zero–sum game," is "opportunity cost" – "What one has give up or forego in order to do something else." This formulation can be applied very usefully to the "zero–sum" library budget illustration above, but will prove absolutely critical to incorporating library patrons into our heuristic, economic model of reference services. And critical, perhaps, to the survival of reference services scrutinized by unforgiving cost–benefit analyses. To illustrate, a student preparing a research paper confronts a variety of choices. One involves the library, collecting information, and the allocation, or expenditure, of time. The student knows that she must have information to support her thesis and recognizes that the quality and quantity of that information will materially affect her desired outcome–a high grade as well as a quality paper. Among other factors, the student also recognizes that the time spent in sorting relevant information once collected, thinking, organizing, careful writing, editing and attention to the physical presentation will also influence her grade.

Obviously, in this example, time is the medium of exchange. Our student has a finite supply. She knows that time spent searching for and recording information in the library cannot also be used for the other activities needed to produce her paper. Nor can use for the other essential, or non–essential but valuable activities in her life. She must decide how to allocate her time. At the point she determines that time spent on the thinking-writing-production component of her task has become more valuable than time spent on the information collection component, she will redirect her activities in order to "maximize her welfare."

Opportunity cost will also determine our student's choice of research methodology and sources. Braunstein suggests that "The cost to the user depends on the value of his time (the opportunity cost), the convenience and efficiency of the library and his efficiency in using the library's collection or in making his needs known to the librarian."

Even if she knows that searching *Psychological Abstracts* will lead to more sophisticated research and more complete coverage of her topic our student will consider how much more time and effort that search will consume, the likely benefit of that search, and then compare her estimates (if only intuitively) to the cost and likely benefit of a quicker, easier, if admittedly less elegant, search in *Social Sciences Index or Expanded Academic Index.*

In view of the high cost of reference services, the zero–

sum nature of library budgets, consumer choice and the growing demand for accountability in the expenditure of public funds, Braunstein has argued that " . . .it is important to examine the costs and benefits associated with each of the feasible alternatives so that one might understand how choices are made." This brings us to two of the policy analyst's and economist's favourite tools: cost-efficiency analysis and cost–benefit analysis.

Cost-efficiency studies seek to determine the least costly (i.e., most efficient) method of achieving a desired outcome, or to determine which of two or more organizations achieve an acceptable outcome at the least cost. In reference services, such analyses might be applied to determine the most efficient means of answering reference questions. They may address the level of personnel used to answer questions or the methodology, for example manually searching an index as compared to the costs, speed and results of a computerized search.

Reports on studies of this type appear in the literature with considerable frequency and can be very useful in problem solving. While cost-efficiency studies employ relatively straightforward methodology and are far more feasible than cost–benefit studies, they still pose significant obstacles. For example, what exactly are the costs involved in answering reference question? They clearly include the wages of the librarian or staff member, but are those wages of the time during which the question is addressed? What about the "dead" time between questions? Shouldn't that be charged as a "cost" in answering questions? But, then how do we account for the reference librarian awaiting questions at the desk at the same time she is also doing general book selection, preparing a book talk for the branch's Wednesday reading group, or writing an article for publication? Surely these activities should not be charged as part of the cost of answering the next reference question.

And then there are all those books, periodical indexes, CD–ROMs. How much of the cost of an encyclopedia should be charged to "answering reference questions?" The librarian will certainly use it to provide a direct answer. But, patrons would also use the same encyclopedia independently and quite satisfactorily without the assistance of a librarian. It is readily apparent that the previous paragraph isn't going anywhere. The next part of that argument probably has something to do with the number or angels that can dance on the head of a pin. That is, in fact, the point. Determining exactly what costs to attribute to which function is extremely complex and almost always arguable. That choice and how those costs are calculated, will radically affect the outcome of the study.

Murfin provides a thorough review of this issue and offer valuable insights into "The most accurate, fair and sensible method of arriving at unit costs for the reference question. . . ."

Even when costs are calculated consistently in comparing processes or institutions, it is difficult to draw conclusions from research conducted in libraries other than one's own–generalizations are limited. Cummings notes that in his study of college libraries for the Council on Library Resources, Kantor found considerable variation in costs associated with monographs acquisitions.

> Selection costs ranged from less than $1.00 per item considered to $4.00. Search costs were as low as $0.25 per item and as high as $3.50. Ordering costs ranged from below $1.00 to more than $5.00 per item.

With only a single investigator, it is very likely that

Kantor's methodology remained consistent across the various libraries even if one might want to argue with how he assigned costs. Observing such variability in the findings, it is difficult to conclude what might be appropriate selection, search and ordering costs. In his efficiency analysis of answering reference questions using paper sources vs. on–line, Anderson gave voice to the frequent frustration encountered by readers of cost–efficiency studies:

> Accurate dollar values in this area are extremely difficult to obtain. Surveying the literature leads one to conclude that the only way to be certain of your own processing and storage costs is to do your own study—a time-consuming and expensive technique.

Cost-benefit analysis, on the other hand, attempts to determine whether the outcome of the process is, in fact, worth the cost. A researcher's determination that it is more cost-effective to answer reference questions using electronic tools rather than paper equivalents (e.g., $12 per question electronically vs. $14 per question using paper tools) should lead to greater use of the electronic media. On the other hand, a finding that the "value" to patrons of a correctly answered reference question is only $10, might, rationally, cause the organization to consider reallocating resources now spent answering reference questions in order to better serve patrons. Recall both opportunity cost and the zero-sum nature of library budgets.

Infact, cost-benefit approach to the evaluation of library services is a logical response to the demands of accrediting bodies that colleges and universities assess outcomes of the educational process. It could also prove an effective tool in responding to citizen calls for greater accountability in the expenditure of government funds. Unfortunately, all the issues making the results of cost-efficiency studies ambivalent and expensive work their same, inhibiting magic on cost-benefit studies.

Besides , cost-benefit analysis is made even more daunting by the extreme difficulty of accurately identifying and valuating the benefit derived from library services. That public, school, special, and academic libraries are beneficial individually and collectively to society seems, at the very least, self-evident. At least to us. We can certainly name and describe some of the benefits. But, can we define them with enough specificity and concreteness to measure them?

Can we approximate the benefit a patron derives from correct answers to reference questions? How might we measure the benefit of reference service? If it is difficult to accurately and consistently ascribe the cost of library services to its various components, how much more difficult must it be to define the benefits? Lancaster recently offered one answer in commenting that "Cost-benefit analyses are very difficult to perform in the information service environment and perhaps no study of this kind has ever been fully credible."

We seem trapped. We've acknowledged that libraries and their reference services are expensive. There seems to be ample evidence that parent institutions, taxpayers, and society in general expect greater accountability for the expenditure of public funds, and that librarians need to better apply the tools of economics to analyzing our operations.

At the same time, the use of those tools presents a steep, long, and, as a result, expensive learning curve while the results we can expect from the application of sophisticated techniques such as cost-efficiency analysis and cost-benefit analysis appear ambivalent. One solution, though certainly incomplete and lacking in absolute answers, may be found in the heuristic application of economic thinking to our understanding of reference services.

Models

Many systems and processes at work in the world are either too large or too complex to understand directly. To clarify our grasp of the whole, social scientists and economists frequently construct simplified, theoretical representations—or models—of social processes. Models have been used to illustrate communications within organizations, how people make decisions, and to forecast the weather. Econometric models provide mathematical formulas which assist economists in predicting future business trends and the condition of the economy on the basis of selective data currently available.

Social and econometric models are, after all, just models. As scaled-down representations of far more complex realities their predictive and explanatory powers are severely limited, equally "scaled-down." Relationships presented in models can only approximate reality, some factors are invariably overlooked or the relationships misunderstood. In addition, the accuracy and quality of data determine and limit the predictions and explanations provided by "modeling." No matter how accurately a model of business cycles might express cause and effect, inaccurate factory inventory data will produce faulty predictions for future business cycles. Garbage in, garbage out.

Toward a Heuristic Model of the Economics of Reference Service

To construct and apply aspects of the model, we will first assemble and define the building blocks called variables.

Even though we have little expectation of giving accurate values to these variables we can still use them heuristically, to help us think.

Now we will come to reference practice in libraries.

Reference Practice

Patrons, readers, consumers, customers, clients, and *users*-all librarians can remember staff debates about the most appropriate term for people who seek material in libraries! The inevitable conclusion of these debates is that no term appears to be entirely satisfactory. As we move into an era where electronic information becomes more dominant, the lack of agreement on terminology for clientele may reflect our uncertain relationships with people we assist. To many librarians, *patron*, with its origins in wealthy nobility who founded and supported private libraries, and *reader*, which implies users of printed materials but not multimedia, reflect the past. *Patrons* and *readers* were more appropriate when libraries were used exclusively by a highly educated elite and composed almost exclusively of printed materials. The terms, *consumers* and *customers*, lack appeal to many librarians as these terms are seen as appropriate for people who are *purchasing* services or products, whereas information access without fees is an important service principle for many public and academic librarians. Many librarians may be particularly reluctant to apply the term, *customer*, to our clientele because libraries in the public sector have a particularly complex relationship with their various constituents.

Unlike private industry, their services are only indirectly tied to revenues- the public decision makers who have to be convinced of the value of library services are generally not the consumers of the library's services. The consumers may have very little influence over funding of library services. As consumers' demands increase, funding may not follow. However, the use of the term, *customer,* might imply the establishment of a more positive relationship with citizens.

Customers are not viewed as passive recipients of uniform services who have very little influence, but rather people actively involved in the process of deciding what would be provided, when, and how. In contrast, *clients*, generally have been seen as people in a less involved, less active role, who are heavily dependent upon the professional expertise of the staff. *Customer* might be the most appropriate term for future library clientele. In an information age, when information is increasingly viewed as a valuable commodity, libraries may be competing directly with private information services for business.

Typical of those with whom libraries may expect to compete in the future is Ameritech. The Ameritech annual report states, "Customers are at the center of everything we do and at the heart of every decision we make. In an age where libraries might no longer survive simply because they are an important public good, the profession can learn much from the customer service movement in the business community.

Through discussion of service encounter and Total Quality Management concepts, this paper will highlight customer service research and practices in business and explore the implications of these movements for reference services.

In fact, the term, service encounter, is now widely used to describe the moment of interaction between the customer and the service organization. In service encounters both customers and service providers, such as reference librarians, have roles to enact. Unlike manufactured goods, a service product is usually produced with customer involvement. The customer often serves as the co-producer of the final service product. In a library setting, the customer will work with the library staff and the library system to produce a final product which is generally enhancement of knowledge, skills, or enjoyment of leisure activities. Service encounters are of great interest in the business world because the bottom line is a fundamental belief that service behaviours are ultimately tied to valued outcomes, such as sales and customer satisfaction.

Research on customer service encounters can be found in a variety of disciplines, psychology, sociology, communication, and business, particularly in retailing, marketing, and management.

Context

Ford and Etienne discuss the importance of context variables such as busyness, products and services matching customer needs, customers' willingness to spend sufficient time with providers, non-monetary (e.g., effort, convenience) factors in customer decisions, and support received from co-workers.

These variables sound both familiar and relevant to reference librarians who interact with customers. Bunge and Murfin have even identified a syndrome of factors generally associated with reference service in libraries reporting lower rates of customer success-some of these factors include context variables summarized by Ford and Etienne.

Behaviour

Remarkably and Etienne also discuss the importance

of behaviours in the customer interaction. They classify behaviours used by service providers into three broad categories: (1) courteous service, such as positive emotions, friendliness, immediacy, sociability, attentativeness, touching, or smiling; (2) personalized service directed at determining and meeting the customer's unique needs; and (3) manipulative behaviours relying on deception or control over customer behaviours. Bunge and Murfin, Durrance, and Dyson identify courteous and personalized service behaviours associated with important service outcomes.

Ford and Etienne's third category- manipulative behaviours- may on first thought appear more relevant to a sales situation where providers wish to persuade customers to purchase products or services rather than a library situation where service is generally provided without fees. However, all reference librarians can certainly identify interaction where they have worked with customers and persuaded them to change their needs to match what the reference librarian can easily and quickly obtain from the library system. In these instances have we fully informed our customers of the main alternatives that exist beyond the library system? When librarians encourage customers to accept what is readily available in the system, how often do customers feel their needs were met?

Examining memorable critical incidents would be useful in exploring instances in which library system constraints rather than customer needs appear to dominate the service interaction. Customer behaviours and demographics may also influence provider behaviours: research indicates that providers may be influenced by customer gender, dress or status, race and weight, and how demanding, sociable, aggressive or involved customers are in their service encounters.

One of the most interesting findings reported is that successful salespersons were those who appeared to be adapting to, and reflecting the sociability of the individual customer; as customers became more aggressive, providers were less likely to perceive their requests as legitimate and less likely to honor their requests. Customers can be beneficial to organizations by recommending the organization to others, replacing materials knocked off shelves and reporting unsafe conditions to employees.

Or customer discretionary behaviour can be harmful, such as stealing materials from organizations. Customer discretionary behaviour would be an interesting service outcome to employ as well as other measures: customer satisfaction success, finding needed materials, and willingness to return. The impact of customer behaviour on reference service has not been systematically explored. Our strongly held philosophical beliefs in equity of reference service to all people (sometimes interpreted as uniform service to all) may make this a difficult area to explore.

Total Quality Management

Total Quality Management (TQM) is best viewed as a management philosophy which combines the teachings of W. Edwards Deming and J. M. Juran on statistical process control and group solving processes with Japanese values concerned with quality and continuous improvement. TQM has become increasingly popular in the United States and Europe during the 1980s, most likely as a result of the success of Japanese firms in a number of global markets.

A major underlying impetus for adopting TQM processes

in the private sector has been competition and survival. Yet, in the public sector, it is hard to appreciate the notion of competition, because we typically see government entities as being the sole provider of unique services. However, changes in technology have made it possible for private information vendors to compete in significant ways with libraries.

Although there is no universal set of TQM principles, Bowen and Lawler have provided a typical listing: (1) Focus on the customer; (2) Quality Work the First Time; (3) Strategic Holistic Approach to Improvement; (4) Continuous Improvement as a Way of Life; and (5) Mutual Respect and Teamwork. These broad principles provide a good framework for discussing the TQM movement and its implications for libraries.

To the customer, value is the benefits received for the burdens endured, such as price, an inconvenient location, unfriendly employees, or an unattractive service facility. Quality service helps an organization maximize benefits and minimize burdens for its customers. Thus, critical to an effective quality process are: (1) thorough identification of customers; (2) their principal service expectations; and (3) a detailed analysis of key work processes that deliver the services.

James Swiss had identified two factors which may make the TQM focus on customers difficult for libraries operating in a public non-profit environment. First, in the public sector the conflict between the programme's direct customers (immediate users) and its ultimate customers general public; taxpayers) can be acute: General taxpayers may prefer to minimize costs while direct customers may expect a level of quality found only at a very high cost. Second, the focus on customer needs and wants may be less effective in the rapidly changing high technology environment of library reference services.

The conventional TQM wisdom that companies should find out what their customers want and use that information to deliver superior quality may work best in situations where customers have stable and well formed preferences. In rapidly changing situations with unstable and uncertain customer preferences, giving customers what they want may not be an effective strategy. Instead, organizations should invest more effort in gaining understanding of various factors influencing actual customer decisions, such as alternatives under consideration, and the manner in which alternatives evaluated.

Understanding how customers make choices in meeting their information needs will assist reference librarians in designing future services of interest to their customers.

Quality Work the First Time

Pursuing quality through TQM requires eliminating or reducing mistakes in the processes organizations use to deliver service. TQM has its roots in statistical control. A key feature is the identification, collection, and use of reliable data for decision making. Data is used as feedback to measure progress towards continuous improvement. The purpose of analyzing data is to identify where variation exits in a process and what causes it. A process "in control" is stable and predictable. Traditional statistical tools for quality improvement are: cause-and-effect diagrams, checklists, Pareto charts, control charts, flow charts, histograms, and scatter diagrams. These TQM tools are useful in displaying data and identifying trends regarding internal library operations.

For libraries, the traditional TQM tools may be most

useful in analyzing and improving automated reference systems which are an increasingly important component of reference service. In analyzing the processes involved in the service encounter, traditional TQM statistical tools do not appear to be as useful as other methods. TQM is very much a product of statistical quality control and industrial engineering. Early applications of TQM were for assembly line work and other routine processes.

With services, controlling variation and producing services with predictable outcomes is often more difficult. For example, Hebert found that there was a wide range of responses in the way staff dealt with interlibrary loan requests, creating great variability in service which is difficult to control. Customers are also a source of uncontrollable variation which may limit the usefulness of traditional TQM tools.

Olzak notes that reference librarians instinctively minimize reference transaction times because customer arrival rates are unpredictable; devoting too much time to one patron shortchanges others and/ or shifts the burden of providing reference services to other departmental members. Services are normally delivering benefits to customers by a system during a process that involves the customer as a co-producer. However, the typical quality programme places considerable effort on improving internal processes of the organization. In using TQM statistical process tools, the organization may lose sight of benefits to the customer as the primary goal.

The link between customer perceived quality and internal process quality may be weak if quality programmes do not start by identifying customer needs and wants-Are we doing the right thing in the eyes of the customer? For example our internal processes may be wonderfully efficient in interlibrary loan, but may not address customer needs. In analyzing the reference service encounter, traditional TQM tools may only be useful after data has been collected that goes far beyond traditional reference statistics. Aluri fails to provide a customer focus when he suggests using traditional TQM tools to analyze transaction data collected only by reference librarians. Relying solely on staff data tends to focus on information which is often more important to librarians than to customers. A method of data collection which is more focused on customers would be to ask both customers and librarians to identify areas where transactions could be improved; then, as a second step, use traditional TQM tools to analyze the results. In initial efforts to survey customers, organizations ought to capture all aspects of quality service which customers think are important. Therefore, using exploratory techniques first-open ended interviews, focus groups- is essential.

Rating scales are appropriate only as a second step. Berry, Parasuraman and Zeithaml suggest the following methods for building a quality information system: (1) soliciting customer complaints to identify the most common categories of service failure; (2) post transaction surveys- to obtain feedback while the experience is still fresh; (3) customer focus group interviews- to provide a forum for customers to suggest improvements; (4) mystery shopping of service providers- to identify systematic strengths and weaknesses in customer contact service; (5) employee surveys- to identify employee perceived obstacles to improved service; and (6) total market service quality surveys- to identify service improvement priorities.

Once levels of customer perceived quality are known, the information must be used to manage internal processes;

if questions asked on a survey do not link back to specific organizational processes being managed, the data collection effort is not worthwhile. For example, an effort that is not useful in managing organizational processes is collecting customer perspectives on " How friendly are library personnel ?" The results cannot be linked to any library process and will not be helpful. No one will take ownership of the results. Who should become more friendly? Is it the reference librarians? Student shelters? Staff at the directions desk? Circulation desk? Or all of the above?

Burns suggests four steps necessary for researching customer service: (1) Find out what the customer wants; (2) Help set performance indicators; and (3) Monitor performance in relationship to those indicators; and (4) Provide information that will help implement change. Pulse provides an exceptionally detailed list on setting up a customer focus programme which includes five stages: (1) Survey current internal and external customer perceptions through carefully worded questionnaires, carefully structured interviews and focus groups; (2) Set standards in both technical and behavioural terms (e.g., 90% accuracy; ask-did you find what you needed?); (3) Provide prolonged and consistent training and development (e.g., peer coaching); (4) Oversee putting programme into practice permanently with goals to incremental improve; and (95) Consolidate by listening and responding to customers' views.

Although developing data on a nationwide scale may be challenging, at least two instruments- SERVQUAL and RTAI-already provide opportunities for the collection of reference process factors. Parasuraman, Zeithaml and Berry have devised an instrument, SERVQUAL, to measure service quality from the customer perspective. They suggest that service quality from the customer perspective can be defined as the judgement that results when the performance of an actual service is compared to expectations of how such a service should perform. SERVQUAL is a multiple 22 item scale which measures expectations and perceptions of service quality. Quality is measured by comparing the difference between ratings assigned to the 22 paired expectation/perceptions statements. The SERVQUAL in its present form, is intended to ascertain customers global perceptions of an organizations's service quality.

In analyzing findings from SERVQUAL which has been used largely in for profit organizations, Berry, Parasuraman and Zeithaml have concluded that the most important dimensions on which customers judge quality are: (1) reliability- the ability to perform the desired service dependably, accurately, and consistently; (2) responsiveness-the willingness to provide prompt service and help customers; (3) assurance-employees' knowledge, courtesy, and ability to convey trust and confidence; (4) empathy- the provision of caring, individualized attention to customers; and (5) tangibles-the physical facilities, equipment, and appearance of personnel.

Hebert evaluated the service quality of interlibrary loan by utilizing SERVQUAL as the customer evaluation of service and comparing the results with an objective efficiency measure set by library staff. She found a lack of congruence between library and customer measures of interlibrary loan performance. Her results suggest that internal library measures of success should not be substituted for customer evaluation. She concluded that a major deficiency in current measures such as fill rate, which measures the proportion of actual requests that are met, is that it does not measure the extent to which customers needs are met. A major challenge for libraries and other organizations is to invent appropriate internal measures and rewards that correspond strongly to external customer measures. Hebert found that the same dimensions which were important in for profit industries were important to interlibrary loan customers: The single most important customer dimension of service, reliability, had the most negative performance score. Likewise responsiveness, which ranked as the second highest dimension for measuring quality, ranked second lowest in performance. The greatest gaps between customer expectations and perceptions of actual service were in staff trying to understand customer needs and the library getting the right book the first time.

While SERVQUAL is designed to measure global perceptions of service quality, the Reference Transaction Assessment Instrument (RTAI) can be used to measure service quality at the level of the individual reference transaction. The RTAI, also known as the Wisconsin-Ohio Reference Evaluation Programme, allows each library to compare its survey results with those of libraries of similar size and type for average and top scoring libraries. Process factors, such as busyness and time spent can be correlated with patron success. Patron success is defined as finding exactly what was wanted and being completely satisfied. Because the RTAI is valid and reliable and provides comparable data which can be used to identify libraries with high customer success, for reference services the RTAI can be regarded as valuable in establishing external data for benchmarking, a key process in TQM. Janet Brown used the RTAI, a reference area problem log and a suggestion box to collect customer perceptions on service quality. Her report provides excellent detail on how the RTAI can be used as part of a programme to assess the quality of reference service.

TQM is an organizational strategy that drives an ongoing continuous process, one that requires radical changes in organizational design and day-to-day operations. TQM requires a systems orientation with a view of the whole that includes horizontal relationships between processes. TQM organizations require flat structured designs so that everyone can be close to the customers, constantly gathering information about customers' current and future needs.

A strength of TQM is that it is designed to promote improvement as part of a comprehensive systems approach. In contrast, Library efforts have often been piecemeal and not tied to assessment of customer needs. Few libraries regularly survey their customers, and of those that do, a majority fail to initiate action in response to survey results. In improving reference service, TQM will require a system approach and evaluation of the process as part of the library system.

The reference process is part of a broader system, including the physical environment, communication, reference sources, reference librarians, totality of demands on reference librarians' time, library technology, technical services, staffing resources, management's expectations, parent institution's management policies and practices, and conflicting philosophies and practices of reference services. Any product or service has four distinct aspects: a physical product, the service product, the service environment, and the service delivery.

In reference service, the physical product is generally the tangible information, or recorded knowledge provided; the service product is staff skills and knowledge applied to the query; the service environment is the reference desk, reference automated systems, printed reference sources;

the service delivery is the interaction of librarian with the customer. Customer perspectives on each of these aspects must be sought to obtain the TQM holistic view.

A set of standards should be established for all services. Once the organization has reached these minimal standards, the goal should be continuous improvement. In contrast to goal setting, which measures the degree to which goals are met and creates after the fact measurement, in TQM measurement of improvement is a continual process; the aim is to provide continual feedback which can be used to measure progress toward improving a process. In the process of continuous improvement, technology can be an enormous advantage for doing things faster and with fewer errors. At Ford, the process of continuous improvement has been institutionalized by routinely surveying customers and talking to them in focus groups. Ford checks with their customers regularly regarding their likes and dislikes, problems and complaints, and how other organizations are serving them better.

Ewell notes the similarities between assessment of instruction and TQM; the most effective assessment techniques provide feedback about process effectiveness and can be used to correct detected deficiencies before the process is over. He discusses the "minute paper" which is administered to students at the end of every class period. The most common version asks two questions: (1) What is the most important thing you learned today? and (2) What is the single thing that after today is still most unclear to you? The minute paper promotes continuous customer (student) feedback which can be used by the instructor in preparing the next class. A similar practice can be promoted in the reference process to obtain feedback; two verbal questions might be: (1) Did you find what you needed today? (2) After you have an opportunity to look at the information, will you let me know if you need anything else?

Basically, Quality improvement requires strong worker participation and total organizational commitment. In TQM training of staff is not a fringe benefit: the continuous staff training requirements associated with TQM are great. Managers should focus on developing skills and abilities necessary to support collective responsibility. Team members will need training in customer satisfaction feedback systems, including skills in developing questionnaires, focus group techniques, mail surveys, listening, and conducting surveys. Training must reach far beyond specific job skills, cover problem solving technologies, problem analysis. Statistical process control and quality measurement. International analysis of training costs show that United States corporations spend less on training than do their Japanese and European counterparts. And libraries spend very little of their budget on staff training.

Infact, training does not appear to be a high priority for library organizations. In a recent survey, the recruitment and hiring of qualified personnel topped the list of priorities.. Viewed as less important were the issues of compensation, training, and retention. In a view representative of many library managers, Stephen Zink suggests that the responsibility for acquiring knowledge of information technology is largely a personal one: part of the responsibility for being a professional is to keep current in one's field. He notes that library schools need to make a more concerted effort to provide continuing education for librarians already in the field. Although he observes that administrators must lead by example, he does not suggest that the library organization should have a major fiscal responsibility for continuous training and education of staff.

Staff empowerment throughout the service process is viewed as an important method of improving service quality. Staff empowerment involves letting people use their judgment more. The TQM premise is that reference quality can be best monitored and improved by the people who are most intimately involved in and affected by the process working together as a team. Establishing trust is also important and for this reason Peterson and Hillkirk believe "mystery shoppers" should be avoided because the practice fosters fear and distrust in employees. TQM promotes trust in employees through a fundamental premise that the operational processes of an organization are more often to blame for low quality service than the workers. Some library managers place blame for reference failures on the librarians rather than the system processes.

Use of mystery shoppers or other unobtrusive customers in evaluating reference services may promote distrust and fear, particularly if managers have access to information on the performance of individual reference staff. Teamwork is important in implementing TQM. Reference librarians should spend time in cataloging as well as catalogers spending time at the reference desk. This will reduce barriers to effective teamwork, such as competition, lack of communication, and different priorities.

Implications For Reference Practice

In 1994 American Library Association President Hardy Franklin said, "Service is the heart of our profession... Our customers whether they be students, faculty, or members of the general public - are why libraries exist... We must market our services in a way that assures our libraries are addressing real needs and that our customers current and potential- are aware of the benefits available to them.

Ameritech not only developed a strategy putting customers at the center but went directly to customer groups and asked how they could best address their needs. Ameritech interviews confirmed that, more than ever before, different categories of customers have different requirements- not only in the products and services they want, but in the way they want to do business. In a similar manner, when planning reference services for special populations, libraries will benefit from interviewing different customer groups on a regular basis.

Information from research on the service encounter and Total Quality Management will also assist the profession in the development of reference services more strongly focused on customer perspectives and designed to meet the needs of different groups in our population. Many librarians are reviewing traditional desk arrangements and exploring different methods of providing assistance which might increase the quality of reference service. Context variables such as busyness, services matching customer needs, customer time and effort, and convenience requirements and their links with costumer reports of success must be included in evaluations of innovations in reference assistance.

Provider behaviours clearly play an important role in the quality of service. Behaviours related to courtesy and the constellation of behaviours which recognize the importance of the customer's individual query associated with successful reference service. Using research findings and professional expertise, the *Reference and Adult Services* Division has developed *Behavioural Guidelines for Reference and Information Services.* These *Guidelines* should be thoroughly tested by exploring the associations between each behaviour and customer judgments of quality, including Durrance's measure of satisfaction, willingness to return, and the success measures used by Murfin, Bunge and Gugelchuk. Some of these behaviours will probably be much more significantly linked to customer judgments of satisfaction, success, and willingness to return than others.

The most important behaviours could then be the focus of library training programmes for all reference employees and included in core courses in library education programmes. The principles of the Total Quality Management movement provide us with insights useful in thinking about quality reference service.

The TQM focus on customer service can be a strong challenge to organizations where there is a heritage of the customer having no alternative source of supply, a culture of professional experience and always knowing best, and being always relatively well thought of by the public and thus believing all is well. TQM is not a comfortable fit with the traditional methods of providing reference assistance in libraries. Devising alternative patterns of reference service with a focus on the customer, quality work the first time, a strategic view of the whole library system, continuous improvement, and in an atmosphere of mutual respect and teamwork will be very challenging.

REFERENCES

A. Parasuraman, Valerie A. Zeithaml, and Leonard L. Berry, "Reassess-ment of Expectations as a Comparison Standard in Measuring Service Quality: Implications for Further Research." *Journal of Marketing 58* (January 1994): 111-124.

Aluri, "Improving Reference Service," 220-236.

Anderson, "Budgeting for Reference Services in an Online Age," p. 185.

Anthony M. Cummings, *University Libraries and Scholarly Communica-tion: A Study Prepared for the Andrew W. Mellon Foundation,* (Washington, D.C.: The Association of Research Libraries for The Andrew W. Mellon Foundation, 1992), pp. xvi-xviii.

ARL Statistics, 1992-93, (Washington, D.C.: Association of Research Libraries, 1994), Table 9, "Total Operating Expenditures," p. 59.

Berry, Parasuraman, and Zeithaml, "Improving Service Quality in Amer-ica," 32-52.

Bitner, Booms, and Tetreault, "The Service Encounter," 71-84. An incident should meet four criteria: (1) involving a customer - provider interaction; (2) very satisfying or dissatisfying from the customer's point of view; (3) being a discrete episode; and (4) having sufficient detail to be visualized by the interviewer.

Bowen and Lawler, "Total Quality-Oriented Human Resources Management," 29-41.

Braunstein, "Costs and Benefits of Library Information," p. 81.

Charles A. Bunge and Marjorie E. Murfin, "Reference Questions-Data from the Field, "*RQ* 27 (1987): 15-18.

Clay Carr, "Total Quality Training," *Training* 27 (November 1990): 59-65.

David E. Bowen and Edward E. Lawler III, "Total Quality-Oriented Human Resources Management, "*Organizational Dynamics* 20 (Spring 1992):29-41.

Digest of Education Statistics, 1993, Table 403, p.427. The most recent, comprehensive data available.

Donald E. Peterson and John Hillkirk, *A Better Idea* : *Refining time Way Americans Work* (Boston: Houghton Mifflin, 1991).

Edward E. Lawler III, "Total Quality Management and Employee Involvement; Are They Compatible?" Academy of Management Executive 8 (1994): 68-76.

F.W. Lancaster, *If you want to evaluate your library...* , 2nd ed.,

(Cham-paign, Illinois: Graduate School of Library and Information Science, University of Illinois, 1993), p. 159.

Ford and Etienne, "Can I Help You?" 413-441.

Francoise Hebert, "Service Quality: An Unobtrusive Investigation of Interlibrary Loan in Large Public Libraries in Canada," *Library & Information Studies Research* 16 (1994): 3-21.

G. Gregory Lozier and Deborah J. Teeter, "Six Foundations of Total Quality Management," *New Directions for Institutional Research* 78 (Summer 1993): 5-11.

J. Stewart and M. Clarke, "The Public Service Orientation: Issues and Dilemmas, "*Public Administration* 65 (Summer 1987): 161-177.

James E. Swiss, "Adapting Total Quality Management (TQM) to Government; "Public *Administration Review 52* (July/August 1992): 356-362.

Jan Mattson. "Improving Service Quality in Person-to-Person Encounters: Integrating Findings from a Multi-disciplinary Review," *The Services Industries Journal* 14 (January 1994): 45-61.

Janet Dagnenais Brown, "Using Quality Concepts to Improve Reference Services," *College & Research Libraries* (May 1994): 211-219.

John Pulse, "Customer Focus: The Salvation of Service Organizations," *Public Library Journal* 6 (1991): *1-5*.

Jurow, "Tools for Measuring and Improving Performance," 113-126.

Kantor summed unit costs over 32 libraries and found" ... that 50% of the total budget eventuates in service as in-house use of library materials." It is important to note that Kantor assumed that "This is presumably not true at public libraries." Paul B. Kantor, "Cost and Productivity in Library Operations," in *Pro-ductivity in the Information Age. Proceedings of the 46th ASIS Annual Meeting,* vol. 20, (Washington, D.C.: American Society for Information Science, 1983), p. 298.

Kordupleski, Rust, and Zahorik, "Why Improving Quality Doesn't Improve Quality," 82-95.

Kordupleski, Rust, and Zahorik, "Why Improving Quality Doesn't Improve Quality," 82-95.

Kordupleski. Rust, and Zahorik, "Why Improving Quality Doesn't Improve Quality," 82-95.

Lancaster, *If you want to evaluate your library...* , p. 304.

Lawler, "Total Quality Management and Employee Involvement, " 68-76.

Leonard L Berry, A. Parasuraman, and Valerie A Zeithaml, "The Service Quality Puzzle," *Business Horizons* (September-October 1988): 35-43.

Leonard L. Berry, A. Parasuraman, and Valerie A. Zeithmal, "Improving Service in Quality America: Lessons Learned, "Academy of Management Executive 8 (1994): 32-52.

Loney and Bellefontaine, "TQM Training," 85-95.

Loney and Bellefontaine, "TQM Training," 85-95.

Lozier and Teeter. "Six Foundations of Total Quality Management," *5-11.*

Lydia Olzak, "Mistakes and Failures at the Reference Desk," *RQ* 31 (Fall 1991): 39-49.

Mairead Browne and Susan Edwards. "How Users Assess the Quality of an Information Service," in Peter Clayton and Russell McCaskie, eds., *Priorities for the Future* (Deakin, Australia: Australian Library and Information Associa-tion, 1992).

Martin Cummings, *The Economics of Research Libraries,* (Washington, D.C.: Council on Library Resources, Inc., 1986), p. 7.

Martin Cummings, *The Economics of Research Libraries,* p. 25.

Martin cummings, *The Economics of Research Libraries,* p. 77.

Mattson, "Improving Service Quality in Person-to-Person Encounters," 45-61; J. Joseph Cronin, J. and Steven A. Taylor, "SERVPERF Versus SERVQUAL: Reconciling Performance-Based and Perceptions-Minus-Expecta-tions Measurement of Service Quality." *Journal of Marketing 58* (January 1994): 125-131.

Miriam A. Drake and Harold A. Olsen, "The Economics of Library Innovation," *Library Trends* 28 (Summer 1979): 102.

Muffin, "Cost Analysis of Library Reference Services," pp. 1-14. See also, Anderson, "Budgeting for Reference Services in an Online Age," pp. 185-186.

Nancy A. Can House and Thomas A. Childers, "The use of Public

Library Roles for Effectiveness, "*Library & Information Science Research* 16 (1994): 41-58.

Nancy A. Van House, Beth T. Weil. and Charles R. McClure, *Academic Library Performance: A Practical Approach* (Chicago: American Library Associa-tion. 1990).

Peter T. Ewell, "Assessment and TQM: In Search of Convergence," *New Directions for Institutional Research* 71 (Fall 1991): 39-52.

Rao Aluri, "Improving Reference Service: The Case for Using a Continu-ous Quality Improvement Method," *RQ* 33 (Winter 1993): 220-236.

Raymond E. Kordupleski, Roland T. Rust, and Anthony J. Zahorik, "Why Improving Quality Doesn't Improve Quality or Whatever Happened to Market-ing?" *California Management Review 35* (Spring 1993): 82-95.

Richard M. Hodgetts, Fred Luthans, and Sang M. Lee, "New Paradigm Organizations: From Total Quality to Learning World Class, "*Organizational Dynamics* 22 (Winter 1994): 5-19.

Shauglmessy, "Benchmarking, Total Quality Management, and Libraries," 7-12.

Susan Jurow, "Tools for Measuring and Improving Performance," *Journal of Library Administration* 18 (1993): 113-126.

Swiss, "Adapting Total Quality Management (TQM) to Government, 356-362.

Swiss, "Adapting Total Quality Management (TQM) to Government," 356-362.

Thomas A. Myers, *An Analysis of Perceived Customer Contac: Service Quality in the Public Sector* (D.P.A. dissertation. Virginia Commonwealth Uni-versity, School of Community and Public Affairs, 1990).

Thomas W. Shaughnessy, "Benchmarking, Total Quality Management' and Libraries." *Library Administration & Management* 7 (Winter 1993): 7-12.

Tim Burns, "Researching Customer Service in the Public Sector," *Journal of the Market Research Society* 34 (1992): *53-60.*

Tim Loney and Arnie Bellefontaine, "TQM Training: The Library

Service Challenge, "*Journal of Library Administration* 18 (1993): 85-95.

U.S. Department of Education, Office of Educational Research and Improvement, National Center for Education Statistics, *Digest of Education Sta-tistics, 1993,* (Washington, D.C.: Government Printing Office, 1993), Table 408, p. 432.

W. Paul Vogt, *Dictionary of Statistics and Methodology: A Nontechnical Guide for the Social Sciences,* (Newbury Park: Sage Publications, 1993), p. 160. For more in-depth discussion of "opportunity cost" from an economist's perspec-tive see McKenzie, "The Economist's Paradigm," p. 10.

Wendy S. Zabara ford and Christina Nathan Etienne, "Can I Help You? A Framework for Interdisciplinary Customer Service Encounters," *Management Communications Quarterly* 7 (May 1994): 413-441.

William Safire, *Safire's Political Dictionary,* (New York: Random House, 1978), p. 808. The concept was popularized and expanded in Lester C. Thurow's *The Zero-Sum Society: Distribution and the Possibilities for Economic Change,* (New York: Basic Books, 1980).

Yale M. Braunstein, "Costs and Benefits of Library Information: The User Point of View," *Library Trends* 29 (Summer 1979): 80.

3

Special Reference Services

> "By competition the total amount of supply is increased and by increase of the supply a competition in the sale ensue, and this enables the consumer to buy at lower rates. Of all human powers operating on the affairs of mankind, none is greater than that of competition."
>
> —*Henry Clay*

In the preceding chapter we have discussed reference service in libraries in the context of practice and economics.

In this chapter we shall discuss library services in two special context i.e. for senior citizens and persons with disability.

Basically, the purpose of library reference service is to answer patrons' questions. Achieving this goal may require explaining how to use the catalogue or a reference tool, finding the answers to questions ranging from simple directional questions to complex research questions, or giving a library tour. The library usually does whatever needs to be done to answer a question, within the limits of its resources and the abilities of its staff. The only reason for a reference service is to help patrons. Reference work requires a desire to serve people; not every LMTA (and, for that matter, not every librarian) is temperamentally suited for reference work.

The LMTA's role in reference service is not as clearly defined as is the role in circulation work and in such technical services as acquisitions, cataloguing, and preparation of materials. In reference service there is no consensus as to how much responsibility can be assumed by the LMTA. Conservative, moderate, and liberal views exist, ranging from one that allows little or no role for the LMTA in reference services to one that gives him a major role. Each library develops the role it will allow its LMTA to assume depending on the attitude of the librarians, the type of library, and the needs of library patrons.

Some responsibilities that the LMTA might assume are staffing information desks, answering directional and ready reference questions, and processing inter-library loans. Most directional questions ("Where do you keep periodicals?") and ready reference questions can be answered by a trained LMTA. In fact, the information desk might be staffed with clerks or student assistants if it has been determined that few questions asked there require an LMTA. Surveys show that in some libraries up to 95% of all questions asked are either directional or ready reference.

Allowing the LMTA to be the patron's first contact will free the librarian from this time-consuming task, which can usually be handled as well by less highly trained staff. In general, it is probably not necessary to insist that the patron's first contact always be with a reference librarian. The major objection to an expanded role for the LMTA is the concern that the quality of reference service will deteriorate. Such deterioration is no more a certainty than it is in medicine and law when paramedics and paralegal personnel are properly used. The selection of staff for reference work is the crucial element in maintaining quality service, and care must be exercised in selecting both librarians and LMTAs.

The most common objection to LMTAs in reference service is that they may attempt to answer questions beyond their ability or training. They may delay too long before referring the questions to a librarian, or they may give a superficial answer and not consult a librarian at all. Although it is possible that poor service might be given occasionally, quality reference service can be maintained and improved, with well-trained and carefully selected LMTAs, because this frees the librarian from the more routine duties.

The author holds a positive view of the role of the LMTA in reference services. The librarian cannot abandon responsibility to provide patrons with quality service. But the librarian also has a responsibility to make the best use of the skills and training of both librarians and the paraprofessional staff. He or she should see that work performed by a librarian is at a professional level and that a professional's talents are not wasted on duties that could be performed by paraprofessionals.

Types

For our purposes, we will classify the questions asked in a reference department into four categories: (1) directional and ready reference, (2) general questions on specific topics, (3) research, and (4) reader's advisory. We will be primarily concerned with ready reference and directional questions because they are the most frequently asked and because the other types should be referred to a librarian. Directional questions require only that the patron be directed to a specific location or to the location of the reference tool that will answer the question.

Typical questions are: "Where is the card catalogue?," "On which floor do you keep current periodicals?," "Where are the restrooms?" All of these questions can be answered with simple directions. The patron can either be told the location, have it pointed out, or be taken there. At a well-staffed information desk or reference desk, questions of this sort will be handled by a paraprofessional, allowing the librarian to make better use of his training.

To answer directional questions satisfactorily, the LMTA must be familiar with the physical layout of the location of various materials. Books are usually shelved in subject order by classification number, and the LMTA should be aware of the locations of books in various classifications. Also, the LMTA must know where periodicals are shelved and how they are arranged. Periodicals are often shelved in a separate section and arranged alphabetically. Some libraries, however, keep current issues of periodicals in one place but catalogue the bound volumes to shelve with the book collection. If the library has other special collections or materials, the LMTA should learn their location. Examples of some of these other materials are pamphlet files, microforms, recordings, art prints, audio-visual equipment, and special collections. While it seems mundane, it is necessary to know the location of restrooms, pencil sharpeners, and vending machines. It takes time to learn about a library, especially about a large library, but it is essential for good reference service.

The answers to ready reference questions are usually short, factual, and easily located in standard reference sources or in the library catalogue. This type of question usually requires little reflection, and the LMTA should be able to think of a source almost immediately. Typical questions might be: "How long is the Mississippi River?,"

"What was the population of New York City in 1960?," "What books does the library have by (or about) John Steinbeck?"

In practice, it is not always easy to distinguish between different types of reference questions. In fact, general reference and research questions, which are discussed below, may start off as directional or ready reference questions. For this reason it is essential that the LMTA analyze each question carefully and refer it to a librarian if there is any doubt about what the patron needs.

A general reference question is one that requires several sources to obtain an answer. Answers may be found in sources other than reference materials, usually including resources found throughout the collection. Typical questions are: "What materials do you have for a paper on Steinbeck?," "What were the causes of World War II?" Obviously these questions cannot be answered by one or two reference sources. Questions of this sort should be referred to a librarian.

Another category of question is the research question. There may be little difference between a research and general reference question except in the number of sources consulted and the depth of the answer.

There may be no definitive "answer" to a research question, and the librarian can only offer a number of references to materials on the subject. The resources of several libraries might be consulted by telephone inquiry or by interlibrary loan if local resources are inadequate. Research questions are always handled by librarians. It is possible, however, that the LMTA might help in answering a research question by searching certain sources preselected by a librarian and by doing some of the bibliographic checking and legwork involved. Another kind of question is the reader's advisory type. Here the patron is seeking material on a particular topic and is interested in suggestions on the "best book" on the subject. In larger libraries a separate reader's advisory department with its own librarian may be established independent of the reference department. In smaller libraries the reference department will handle reader's advisory questions. Answering this kind of question requires skills often quite different from those needed to answer the other kinds of questions discussed above.

In reference work it is often difficult to categorize questions. Nonetheless, the LMTA must analyze questions as well as he can in order to give the best service. This skill can be acquired through experience, preferably under the direction of a skilled reference librarian.

Limits of Reference Service

All libraries place some limits on the reference services they offer. Each library must establish a policy based on its resources, staff, the clientele served, and the purpose of the library. The limits on reference services are usually established by the library's administration and not unilaterally by the reference department. A staff manual or reference manual will clearly define the limitations.

Reference service limits vary greatly among libraries. In a public library the reference service may refuse to answer questions to help patrons do crossword puzzles or to answer contest questions. Restrictions may also be placed on how much help will be given to students working on school projects. An academic library may give limited reference service to students from other institutions. An academic library may also refuse to do translations for students or faculty. In a special library, however, translating may be a common service. Generally no library gives either legal or medical advice, instead referring the patron to a reference source or to a local legal aid service or medical society. The LMTA must be aware when the patron is seeking legal or medical advice and refer the question to a librarian or suggest a reference source or one of the local services mentioned above.

Reference Techniques

The use of "old-fashioned common sense" is the basis for good reference technique. Nearly every book on reference service lists a set of techniques for handing questions based on common sense and respect for the patron. Some of the more important techniques are discussed below.

All questions should be treated as equally important, since the patron would not ask a question unless it was important to him. It is not up to the library staff to decide what is or is not important as long as the question is within the limits of service offered by the library. The librarian may decide to limit the time and staff that can be given to an inquiry, but the LMTA usually does not make this decision.

The patron should be made to feel at ease. Patrons are often intimidated and are afraid of looking foolish. Staff at the information or reference desk should look approachable. In this chapter we will discuss reference services, the purpose of reference work, and the role of the LMTA in a reference departments if they are there to serve the patron. It is unfortunate that patrons begin an inquiry with, "I am sorry to bother you, but . . ." When the LMTA is so busy doing something else that a questioning patron does indeed disturb him, the patron's timidity is reinforced. A person surrounded by work hardly presents the image of being there to serve the patron. Many jobs can be performed at slow periods, but the person at the reference desk should not seem too busy to answer questions. A smile and a pleasant word will go a long way toward putting the patron at ease, especially since many patrons are reluctant to ask a question in the first place.

Staff at the reference desk should listen carefully to the patron's question in order to determine exactly what the patron wants; unfortunately, patrons often are unclear when asking for information. One must remember that the question is important to the patron or he or she would not bother to ask it. During the process of listening to the question, the LMTA should be trying to determine whether the question is directional, ready reference, or one that should be referred to a librarian.

Another reference policy is to treat questions as a private matter between the patron and the library staff member. The patron's inquiry is not the concern of other patrons or even other staff, unless it is necessary to refer the question. A patron who asks a question is, in a way, placed in an "inferior" position. This may be the feeling that makes some patrons reluctant to approach library staff with any question, and library personnel must be careful to avoid giving the impression of being "superior." Since many patrons do not like to be placed in the position of having to ask another person for help, library personnel must remember this when they deal with patrons. Except for blatant rudeness, few things will discourage a person faster than the feeling of being patronized. There is little place in a public services operation for staff who consistently show that they feel "superior," and thereby discourage patrons.

Ageing is a growing phenomenon. All over the world a major section of population is gradually aheading old age. In 1990, there were 53 million Americans over the age of 55, 31.6 million of whom were over age 65. One in every eight Americans is over the age of 65, making the older adult population of the U.S. greater than the entire population of Canada. The American Association of Retired Persons (AARP), which admits to membership anyone over the age of 50, has over 30 million members, and has become a political force of enormous power. This is hardly surprising, given that people over 65 control two in five consumer dollars and almost one in three federal budget dollars is spent for their benefit.

Couple this with the fact that 20% of voters are seniors and that Americans age 55-74 have had the highest voting rates in last five national elections, and it is not difficult to understand the attention politicians give to the concerns of older adults. The sheer numbers provide a compelling argument for library services for the group of older adults, but there are dangers inherent in identifying individuals as group members. The tendency to think in terms of stereotypes or averages is overwhelming. Yet effective library service is based on awareness of the needs of the individuals. So while we may think of the "average" older adult as having 12 years education, being married and living with a spouse in a home which they own, having an income in the low $20,000s, a savings account, life insurance, and no debt and who retired by choice at age 63, that precise profile fits only a minority of group members. Sociologists recognize groups within the group: ethnic minorities, rural populations, prisoners, women, and the "vulnerable elderly" or "old old." Such diversity in the older adult population merely reflects the diversity within library communities.

The current emphasis on community analysis, appropriate planning, and targeted marketing draws attention to specific groups; the unswering commitment to serve all patrons provides a foundation for effective library service. Services to older adults, as service to all special populations and specific groups, draw from a common, service philosophy based on lifelong learning.

Learning Patterns of Older Adults

The greatest barrier to full participation for older adults is often ageism. Myths about the horrors and sadness of growing old permeate American thinking, yet studies indicate that such ideas are unfounded. Older adults learn better, live more independently, are more active, and are healthier and safer than is generally realized. Lifelong learning is a widely recognized phenomenon, and support for lifelong learning theory draws from a variety of disciplines, including education, sociology, psychology, and management and business administration. Librarians with a commitment to providing services to older adults will find they have much in common with other service professionals. Waters and Goodman, in their book, *Empowering Older Adults: Practical Strategies for Counselors,* target "the 95 percent of older persons who live in the community and wish to remain independent as long as possible" and work from the conviction that "older adults can learn, change, and take control of their lives.

Obviously, learning is a process that may continue from birth to the grave, provided that the learning process is established, positive attitudes are developed, and opportunities are provided to encourage continued growth. While learning patterns of older adults may be different from those of younger people, there is significant evidence to support the claim that adults continue to learn effectively throughout the lifespan. Older adults tend to have greater wisdom-that is, assimilate learning into a context based on broader experience.

Verbal skills seem to increase with age, while mathematical skills appear to decline. Older adults generally work more slowly and do poorly in times tests, but often commit fewer errors because they avoid a trail and error approach. Research on learning patterns suggests that adults demonstrate learning preferences that are markedly different from the typical pedagogical approach. Adults prefer to control the pace of learning activities, to learn independently, to use discussion to reinforce and stimulate ideas, and generally to take a more active and controlling part in the learning activities in which they are engaged.

The greatest factor affecting continued learning is not age, but a personal predisposition developed over the course of a lifetime. Turock, however, notes that despite the significant body of research to the contrary, "it remains a fact that librarians subscribe to the myth of an intellectual decline in aging." Her series of studies tracing the development of public library services to older adults leads her to conclude that the provision of services has not kept pace with the growth of older populations, a finding reinforced by several other researchers. It should be noted, however, that these studies tend to focus on specialized services to older adults, and may not reflect the level of service provided by librarians who have chosen a more integrated approach to service provision.

ALA Guidelines for Service

ALA documents demonstrate that some segments of the library community, most notably the RASD Library Service to an Aging Population Committee and ASCLA's

Library Service to the Impaired Elderly Forum, have been aware of the need for services to older adults. Two documents in particular will provide guidance for those implementing or expanding services to older adult populations.

"The Library's Responsibility to the Aging, "developed by RASD's Library Service to an Aging Population Committee, was first adopted in 1964 and revised in 1970, 1971, and 1981. This very brief document offers ten broad areas in which librarians may offer service, beginning with "contributing toward to positive attitude toward aging and the aged."

The 1987 "Guidelines for Library Service to Older Adults" prepared by the Library Services to an Aging Population Committee of RASD supersedes the 1975 "Guidelines for Library Services to an Aging Population." These guidelines provide specific activities for accomplishing service goals, and will prove invaluable in planning services to older adults. This document in many ways parallels the earlier "Responsibility" document, but provides much greater detail.

Library services for older adults have essentially the same goals as services for all of our patrons-to provide the means for enriched leisure, the information for effective living, and the opportunity for continued growth and learning throughout the entire lifespan. The specific articulation of these services will vary according to the community's needs and demands. The difficulty is in ensuring that the special needs of older adults are met while remembering that "an older adult has a range of interests and abilities similar to any adult, and that . . . it is imperative that our programmes be entirely free of any condescending nuances associated with aging."

Public services librarians already possess the skills necessary for successful interaction with older adults. They are accustomed to dealing with diverse clienteles with varying levels of education, different information needs, and unique personalities. The essential component is attitude. Reference librarians must be alert to special needs, while avoiding a paternalistic attitude on one hand or an abrupt and impatient approach on the other.

Self-awareness is the first step, and librarians should begin by examining their own attitudes to ensure that they have not unconsciously accepted stereotypes about older adults, whether those stereotypes are positive or negative. Providing special guidelines for interaction with older adults must be viewed with some trepidation. Most older adults will require no special treatment, and providing techniques for those who do tends to reinforce stereotypes and lead to inappropriate generalizations.

Nevertheless, a few suggestions may enhance awareness. Special techniques required for interviewing older adults are relatively simple.

An interview with an older adult may take more time for a number of reasons. Studies indicate that as people age they may become more internally directed, more egoistic, and less concerned about the opinions of others, so they may feel less inclined to come to the point and hurry along just for the convenience of others. Learning theory also suggests that older adults are more likely to take time to fully understand situations and tasks before beginning, while younger people may prefer immediate action and a trial and error approach.

Many older adults also develop a more relaxed attitude toward time; they slow down and genuinely enjoy and savor life in a way they couldn't when their lives were governed by timeclocks, carriers, and family responsibilities. They may also view their trips to the library as opportunities for socialization, and they may actually enjoy visiting with the staff. Recognition of these factors will not help the busy librarian eliminate the situation, but it may help with acceptance and understanding of the patron's needs.

Nolan's article, "Closing the Reference Interview: Implications for Policy and Practice," provides an excellent overview of factors influencing the length and success of reference interviews. Public services librarians will find the section on establishing reference goals and objectives particularly useful, and will want to consider the needs of older adults in reviewing their own expectations for reference transactions.

Most older adults will require no special treatment. Some, however, will be reluctant to ask for help they need for fear of seeming troublesome or demanding. The librarian will need to be doubly conscientious in confirming that the patron's needs have been met by asking closing questions such as "Is this what you needed?" or "May I do anything else for you?" and articulating a willingness to help- "Please don't hesitate to ask if you need anything else."

As a result of the Americans with Disabilities Act (ADA), may public services librarians are becoming more skilled in meeting the special needs of patrons. Gradual loss of vision and/or hearing are a part of the aging process, though most older patrons don't consider themselves "disabled." They might be "slowing down a little bit," a trifle "hard of hearing," or need "bigger print or longer arms."

Some older adults will need service accommodations,

as will some younger people with disabilities. Public services librarians will find it second nature to utilize basic techniques for enhancing the reference interaction. It is rather natural to repeat a comment if a patron leans forward, places a hand behind the ear, looks puzzled, or asks what was said.

Looking directly at the patron, speaking in a measured and clear, but not exaggerated, voice and keeping hands, gum, and hair away from the mouth will also enhance interaction. Keeping a pad and pencil handy for writing notes will help clarify information for all patrons, not just those who have difficulty in hearing. A patron with a visual impairment may need additional service, particularly in libraries that have not met ADA standards for signage. Range signs, the card catalog or OPAC may all be unreadable. A patron who can read regular print with a magnifier may need help in locating the correct volume on the shelf. Some patrons who can read large print books may have difficulty in reading spines, and those who listen to tapes may need help in reading titles.

Again, the accommodation is second nature to most public service librarians; the librarian "points with the feet" by getting out from behind the reference desk and walking with the patron to the stacks. In addition, librarians will find that it is a simple matter to provide enlarged photocopies and a variety of magnifiers for use with reference materials, but that such accommodations result in moire effective reference service for many patrons.

Information and Referral Services

The section above gives some suggestions for interviewing and general guidelines for interacting with older adults. There are a number of important elements in providing adequate information services to older adults.

Coupled with the necessity for a personal attitude that demonstrates respect for older adults and results in treating all patrons with dignity is the need for knowledge of significant information needs and resources for fulfilling them.

Scanning the literature of various fields such as social work, sociology, counseling, gerontology, and medicine is helpful, and there is a great deal to be learned from this activity, but it is time consuming and requires a great deal of synthesis. More effective is using a good basic source, such as Turock's *Serving the Older Adult,* or Casey's *Library Service for the Aging* to become familiar with areas of information need common to older adults. Especially helpful in identifying library resources are Brazil's *Building Library Collections on Aging,* Rubin and McGovern's *Working with Older Adults* and Hudson's *Libraries for a Lifetime. Working with Older Adults: a Handbook for Libraries* (California State Library) and *Libraries for a Lifetime* (Oklahoma Department of Libraries) provide essential background and procedures for librarians wishing to implement older adults services.

Modern Maturity, Mature Outlook and other magazines that are published for the older adult audience and newspaper columns written for seniors help to keep reference librarians aware of issues and may provide current information for vertical files.

Establishing links with other community service agencies will aid in planning programmes, gathering information for vertical files, establishing networks for referral, and developing entries in community information databases. Brochures and catalogs from the National Council of Aging, Inc., and other associations are focused and timely.

Traditional collection development tools are useful for keeping collections current, and some of these will provide special features on resources for older adults. Attending ALA conference programmes offered by RASD's Services to an Aging Population Committee or ASCLA's Library Services to the Impaired Elderly Forum is an interesting and painless way to keep current.

Areas of interest to older adults fall broadly within interest areas of the general adult population, but different specific topics are of primary concern. Listed below are areas in which reference librarians are most frequently called upon to supply information.

Notably, *changing family relationships* are often a cause for concern. Older adults may need information about second marriages, especially if they are recently widowed or if their children feel compelled to become involved in their selection of a spouse. Because of the increased lifespan, many older adults are finding themselves responsible for their own aged parents and may need to know about alternatives for care and mechanisms for social, emotional, and economic adjustments.

Of critical importance to many older adults is maintaining autonomy in the face of concerned and well-meaning children. Because many people have accept the myth that roles become reversed and adult children are required to parent the parent, older adults may need to find ways to accept nurturing without compromising autonomy and integrity. Another area of family relations that has recently found more widespread interest is that of parenting grandchildren. As a result of a number of sociological trends, including drug addiction, single parenting, and teenage pregnancy, a growing number of older adults are finding themselves acting as parents to grandchildren, a responsibility that most did not expect to assume and feel ill-equipped to fulfill.

Health, fitness, and sex absorb the interest of many older adults, reflecting the popular trend common to all age groups. It is predictable that older people have concerns about some specific health problems that become more acute with age: heart disease, Alzheimer's, high blood pressure and stroke, and more recently, prostate and breast cancer. The alert librarian will recognize that conventional information sources and treatments may be geared to younger people. For instance, a recent newspaper article revealed that older women often neglect to conduct regular breast self-examinations because they lack the mobility and vision to do so. An alternative method has been developed, but it is recent enough that the information may not be included in books that provide traditional approaches to women's health. Fortunately, publishers and medical experts appear to be aware of the need for materials targeted for the older adult audience, and titles such as *Ourselves, Growing Older: Women Aging with Knowledge and Power are more* common.

Information on drugs and drug interactions are of vital importance to older adults who want to be informed consumers. Statistics reveal that the typical older adult averages 15 prescriptions annually and is taking six different prescription medicines simultaneously.

It may seem natural that *grieving, death and dying* are important concerns for older adults. Studies report, however, that only 24% of old adults worry about death, as compared to 55% of 18 to 24 year olds. Many older adults take a rather pragmatic view about their own deaths, and want information for estate planning and making funeral arrangements so as to relieve the burden on surviving spouses and children. Seniors may need support and guidance in dealing with loss of a spouse, a child, friends or a pet.

Living arrangements are of primary concern. Librarians can help older adults make intelligent choices by providing information about a wide variety of options, including retirement apartments, nursing homes, and services that enable older adults to maintain independent households. In addition, the Americans with Disabilities Act has heightened awareness, and many of the young old 50-65 years old) are seeking information for remodeling and adapting their homes in anticipation of some of the mobility problems that might arise in old age. Personal safety and security measures are important to older adults, though the image of senior as victim is not a particularly accurate or empowering one.

To sum up, older adults now have time to pursue *leisure activities.* Travel information is of particular and perennial interest. Librarians will want to check their regular sources to ensure that information about senior discounts is included. Hobby information, particularly about sewing and gardening, is popular. Some sources will provide techniques for participating in favourite activities while accommodating problems such as arthritis, rheumatism, oar reduced mobility or vision.

Reader's Advisory Services

The provision of fiction guidance has emerged (again) as a growing part of the reference librarian's opportunity for service. Many older adults continue to use the library for recreational reading, reflecting their own established patterns as well as the general pattern of public library use. As Casey notes, "leisure time is, and probably will continue to be, a challenge for the aged and an opportunity for the library." Reader's advisory interviews provide the opportunity for intellectual stimulation and socialization for both the librarian and the patron, as well as for establishing a foundation of trust for future transactions. Again, librarians will be aware of diverse interests within the older adult population.

Some prefer mystery or romance while others like westerns or anything on the *New York Times* Best Seller Lists. Some will be offended by anything more than a chaste kiss; others will want to know if you have anything "Juicy." Some want graphic true crime novels, others want a genteel murder mystery with no blood. And some patrons will want to read sensitive novels about growing older or will enjoy seeing an older adult as the protagonist in genre fiction. There are a number of excellent tools available to reader's advisors. The best general introductory source on the reader's advisory process is Saricks and Brown's *Reader's Advisory Service in the Public Library,* which provides planning and interviewing strategies. *Genreflecting and What Do I Read Next?* are important bibliographic resources. In additions, genre-specific sources such as Mackler's *Murder by Category* will be of value in serving patrons whose preference is for a certain type of literature. Librarians who want the convenience of sources that concentrate on literature featuring older adults will find Rubin's *Of a Certain Age and* Donavin's *Aging with Style and Savvy* invaluable. Monroe and Rubin's *The Challenge of Aging is* a classic, and older fiction and nonfiction materials may be found here.

These sources are helpful in recommending books and

materials for patrons and serve the valuable secondary function of enhancing the librarian's understanding of the issues and concerns of the older adult population. Booklists, bookmarks, and publicity provided by reader's advisors should be printed clearly, in an uncluttered font and with high contrast between letters and background.

Programming

It is pertinent to note that programming for older adults inevitably receives high marks from participants. Programmes range from those targeted for a general audience but attended by older adults to international programming planned with interaction among age groups as a primary focus to programmes planned exclusively for older adults. Within each of these categories, there exists a wide variety of topics and goals.

While lecture programmes provide information for daily living, formal elderhostel programs offer educational opportunities, book discussions stimulate intellectual activity and socialization, and reminiscence programming encourages older adults to validate their experiences and communicate them to a younger generation.

Informational programmes on current issues are popular among older adults. These topics are in areas of importance throughout the lifespan, but are reflective of the developmental tasks, life changes, and consumer needs of the group. For instance, programmes on financial planning may focus on estate planning or retirement planning; programmes on exercise may emphasize swimming and low-impact workouts; programmes on taxes may include such topics as the effect of a second marriage on social security income and benefits.

Skimming *Modern Maturity,* the magazine of the

American Association of Retired Persons, will keep the librarian abreast of topics of interest to seniors. Older adults often attend the National Endowment for the Humanities (NEH) Let's Talk About It programmes. These discussion programmes, led by humanities scholars, are planned for general audiences, but Durrance and Rubin report on attendance by older adult participants and accommodations made for them.

Silver Editions, the National Council on Aging, Inc. (NCOA) programme series, follows the Let's Talk About it format and are planned around topics designed to appeal to older adult audiences. Evaluation of the NCOA programme provides practical information for programme planners: (1) Participants are generally already library users; (2) Smaller groups (no more than 15 participants) seem to be most effective. Attrition over the span of the series seems inevitable; (3) Factors such as scheduling (daytime preferred), facility (smaller, cozier room with comfortable chairs), and refreshments coffee and desserts) are very important; (4) Brief, but focussed training for presenters enhances success, even if the presenters are experienced educators drawn from universities and colleges. Interestingly, while programme topics are chosen to reflect past experiences and history, comments from participants indicate that older adults are well-informed about current events and open to innovation.

For example, discussions of the internment of Japanese in America during World War II evoked analogies to the then-current treatment of Arabs in America During Desert Storm. Suggestions for ways to improve the programmes included requests for tours and training on online public access catalogs and electronic databases. Reminiscence programming, in which adults reflect on past experiences, are sometimes offered with the aid of Bifolkal kits, which offer scripts, audiovisual aids, and instructions and materials for activities. As with the humanities discussion programmes listed above, these centrally developed programmes are great time severs for local librarians.

Reminiscence programming provides opportunities for socialization and validation, and they are sometimes regraded as bibliotherapy for participants. Some librarians, however, have combined reminiscence programming with oral history projects, thus enhancing local history collections and providing tangible evidence of an appreciation of the value of older adults. Services such as the popular VITA/IRS tax help programme involve older adults on both sides of the desk, as both information providers and recipients. Such programmes offer recognition of the contribution senior volunteers can make.

Many librarians have recognized that older adults can provide valuable service to the library, and seniors are often willing volunteers. While volunteer programmes offer benefits by promoting positive attitudes towards aging and older adults, librarians must remember that it is the library that receives primary benefit from such activities. The notion that libraries are doing older adults a favour by providing opportunities for meaningful activity is condescending and demeaning. Care should be take to follow ALA's *Guidelines for Library Service to Older Adults* regarding use of volunteers.

Outreach, referral, and delivery services are essential elements of service for older adults who are institutionalized or homebound. These services, per se, are not within the purview of this article. It is well to remember, however, that many adults , both young and old, are often hospitalized or temporarily in need of such services. Selecting and reserving materials, adapting service policies that allow family members or other designees to check out materials, and offering flexible eligibility criteria for delivery and books by mail services will ensure continuous service for those with temporary problems.

Librarians will also want to think of outreach in the broader terms of "stimulation," "public relations," and "marketing." Involving older adults in planning for peers promotes effective service. Announcements (in large print) of library services and activities can be placed in appropriate newsletters or posted in retirement communities, nursing homes, local offices of aging councils, churches, or senior centers. As noted earlier, liaisons with other community agencies and local associations will be valuable in informing older adults and care givers of opportunities provided by the library and in predicting the need for library services. Library newsletters and mailings can be made available in large print formats and sent on request, or mailing lists with a "large print" designation can be developed.

It is obvious that older adults are one group among many, and the individuals who comprise that group may belong to other groups as well. Librarians will continue to demonstrate their concerns and to offer service-one patron at a time. Serving older adults is not a matter of developing new and unfamiliar services. It is often not a matter of serving new patrons -just patrons who, for the convenience of demographers, have entered a new classification. It is the application of a bit of specialized expertise to a broad foundation of experience, knowledge, and service. It is a matter of doing the same things we've always done, but with greater sensitivity, more awareness, stronger commitment and enthusiasm. It is, after all, a matter of focus.

Library Services for Disabled Persons

Before coming to the main theme, first an instance. Recently an academically able student at the University of Alabama checked out a book. He did it in the usual way, using he online catalog to locate the call number and a printer to record the location. Yet when the transaction was completed, book in hand, the student broke into a broad smile and announced to nearby patrons and library staff that this was the first time in his life that he had checked out library material on his own. The student is totally blind. He had used adaptive equipment to read the catalog and a Braille printer to print the location and call number; his independence was the result of a year's work on the part of library staff and students with disabilities and a highpoint in an exhilarating, though occasionally discouraging and frustrating, journey. In a sense, the student's smile is a direct consequence of the Americans With Disabilities Act of 1990 (ADA). Among its findings, ADA stated that "census data, national polls, and other studies have documented that people with disabilities, as a group, occupy an inferior status in our society, and are severely disadvantaged socially, vocationally, economically, and educationally. "The purpose of the act is "to provide a clear and comprehensive national mandate for the elimination of discrimination against individuals with disabilities," to provide "enforceable standards against this discrimination," to "ensure that the Federal Government plays a central role in enforcing the standards established in this Act," and "to invoke the sweep of congressional authority.... in order to address the major areas of discrimination faced day-to-day by people with disabilities."

Since the ADA prohibits discrimination in public entities and "public accommodations and services operated by private entities," it relates directly to public and private libraries. Passage of the ADA and an increasing awareness of the needs of persons with disabilities has prompted libraries all over the country to look more carefully at their disabled populations and at the services offered to them. This article will explore the burgeoning body of resources on library services for users with disabilities and then turn to a case study of how one institution, The University of Alabam Libraries, has addressed the mandate of the ADA.

Inevitably the passage of the ADA created an accompanying literature, intended to guide libraries through the maze of ADA implementation and to provide an understanding of the library needs of persons with disabilities. For the most part, these sources fit into four categories: general information on the ADA, information on library compliance with the ADA, library services for special populations, and information on adaptive technologies. The two latter categories, of course, had been discussed before, and were in a sense a part of the pressure for the ADA. Two general sources, *Complying With the Americans With Disabilities Act: A Guidebook for Management and People With Disabilities* by Don Fersh and Peter W. Thomas and *Implementing the Americans With Disabilities Act* by Lawrence O. Gostin and Henry A. Beyer, provide a good basic understanding of the ADA.

Boht cover the history of the act and earlier disability legislation and offer a thorough explanation of the act's titles and terminology, an important inclusion since a new, often confusing, ADA language now exists. Useful also is Gostin and Beyer's section on implications of the ADA for persons with psychiatric, mental, and developmental disabilities, an increasingly prominent group of library users. Library compliance with the ADA is thoroughly covered in *How Libraries Must Comply with the Americans With Disabilities Act (ADA),* edited by Donald D. Foos and Nancy C. Pack. Of particular note are the chapters by Michael Gunde, which explains how the act's titles relate to libraries, and by Ruth O'Donnell, which provides a six-step ADA planning model. *Surveying Public Libraries for the* ADA, a guide to compliance prepared for the Panellas Public Library Cooperative, combines general information with a self-evaluation inventory; belying its title, the survey is helpful to other kinds of libraries as well. Readers may also want to consult a recent ALA preconference publication, *The Americans with Disabilities Act: It's Impact on Libraries The Library's Responses in "Doable" Steps.* And in another clear, concise overview of library compliance, "The Americans with Disabilities Act and its Effect on Public Libraries," Christopher Lewis explains the titles, compliance, enforcement, and deadlines, paying careful attention to physical barriers, equal access to programmes, and weknesses of the ADA (the vague terminology, for example). The literature on library services for persons with disabilities consists of general guides and how-to manuals, descriptive accounts of library programmes, and discussions of the library needs of users with specific disabilities. Ruth Velleman's exceptional overview, *Meeting the Needs of People with Disabilities: a Guide for Librarians, Educators, and Other Service Professionals* includes information on almost every aspect of services to persons with disabilities. Of particular interest are Velleman's discussions of highly specialized library programmes for the disabled and her careful and sensitive treatments of a broad range of disabilities.

Serving the Disabled, by Keith C. Wright and Judith

F. Davie, is a manual offering general information, resource lists, and worksheets on adult and youth programmes, reference services, collection development, and new technologies. The April 1990 issue of Illinois Libraries, edited by H. Neil Kelley, stands out as a valuable comprehensive study of library services for persons with disabilities. It includes articles on the varied services coordinated by Illinet, extending from talking book and television services to story hours for deaf and visually impaired children and programmes for senior citizens. In a similar vein, *Libraries Serving Underserved Populations, an issue of Library Trends,* is devoted to meeting the library needs of the deaf. Chapters over communication with the deaf, collection development for deaf populations, and literature for deaf children.

Malanie Norton's chapter, "Effective Bibliographic instruction for Deaf and Hearing-Impaired College Students" offers techniques for group and individualized bibliographic instruction and suggestions for appropriate handouts. Meeting the library needs of persons with developmental, learning, or mental disabilities is an especially vexed issue. Darlene Weingand, "The Invisible Client," discusses materials and services for the learning disabled at the Westchester, New York Public Library and offers guidelines for other libraries to evaluate their services to this group. Fay Zipkowitz, "No One Wants to See Them': Meeting the Reference Needs of the Deinstitutaionalized, describes the efforts of the Rhode Island Department of State Library Services to bring library service to newly mainstreamed users, while Sally Reed, "Breaking Through: Effective Reference Mediation for Nontraditional Public Library Users, "treats the attitude of the library staff toward users with mental illness, a crucial and sensitive topic.

Since new products appear constantly, information on adaptive technologies will undoubtedly increase in the next few years. Barbara Mates' *Library Technology for Visually and Physically Impaired Patrons* identifies available technologies and their use in a library setting. Although some newer technologies are not included,, Mates' thorough product descriptions, her glossaries and bibliographies, and her extensive lists of vendors and resources make this a highly useful source for those new to the field. John Jax, "Library Services for Students With Disabilities at the University of Wisconsin-Stout,' describes adaptive equipment used for blind, visually impaired and learning disabled students as well as the adaptations made to physical access and furnishings.

Grant and Jones provide a nuts-and-bolts overview of the daunting technology of a voice catalog in "The three T's for a Talking Online Catalog: Technology, Teamwork, Teaching." Developing a programme for users with disabilities is a work-in-progress that needs continual refinement as services are expanded or revised; sometimes information is needed more rapidly than printed publication characteristically permits.

Fortunately guidance is available from national and regional library associations and through the Internet. Through the LITA Adaptive Technologies Interest Group and The Association of Specialized and Cooperative Library Agencies (both groups of ALA), librarians have access to conference programmes, informal discussion groups, and handouts. National and regional conference exhibits also offer the opportunity for hands-on demonstrations of the latest adaptive equipment. Electronically, a growing number of e-mail lists accessed through the Internet or BITNET allow subscribers to share information on particular disabilities, ADA compliance issues, and adaptive technologies.

In addition, an online workshop and a electronic journal are offered through EASI (Equal Access to Software and Information), an organization that operates under the aegis of the American Association of Higher Education. Information about services and resources of The National Library Service for the Blind and Physically Handicapped of the Library of Congress is available through the Library of Congress gopher, LC. Marvel.

CASE STUDY: THE UNIVERSITY OF ALABAMA LIBRARIES

The University of Alabama Libraries serve a large campus community, students and faculty from other local colleges, and the town population. Some users are persons with disabilities. Of course, the University had attempted to meet the needs of the disabled before 1992, the ADA's target year for implementation. The Rehabilitation Act of 1974, the precursor to ADA, prohibited discrimination in programmes or activities receiving Federal financial assistance. Well before ADA, consequently, the University had developed an awareness of its responsibility to the disabled. Much of what might have been supposed to be the University's direct responsibility, however, was borne by the state of Alabama: most disabled students were assisted by the on-campus presence of a state agency, the Office of Disabled-Student Services. The Office hired teaching assistants to serve as readers (for the blind) and interpreters (for the deaf), to retrieve books from library stacks, and otherwise to provide academic assistance. In the years before the passage of the ADA, the libraries installed Braille lettering on elevators and purchased a Kurzweil reader. Except for the Kurzweil, adaptive equipment was not available. Many students came to campus with their own equipment; some simply depended on family or friends for library help. Disabled-Student Services did such a thorough job of handling the library needs of the visually impaired that the Kurzweil was rarely used.

Passage of the ADA created an increased awareness of the needs of disabled persons, in part the result of greater assertiveness of the disabled community. With ADA, the University (hence the libraries) also assumed a new and direct legal responsibility for meeting the needs of the disabled. While the Office of Disabled-Student Services continues to be present on campus, it no longer has primary responsibility for the provision of academic support services. The University and Libraries responded to the new situation with new policies and institutional structures. The hub of the Libraries' efforts was, and remains, the University Libraries Committee on Specialized Access, with responsibility to develop, coordinate and evaluate library services for users with disabilities. Conceived of partly as an advocacy group, the committee included library staff members, faculty and students with disabilities, and representatives from various related campus office. The committee also served initially as a planning body. Through subcommittees, committee members began work on projects related to physical accessibility, staff awareness, public relations, and electronic access. The chair of the University Libraries Committee on Specialized Access also served as part of a campus-wide network of liaisons for the disabled; the Libraries Planning Officer was made part of the University ADA Task Force, an oversight group.

The primary focus of the Libraries' efforts in the first two years has been the establishment of an adaptive technologies laboratory for blind, visually impaired, and learning disabled students. Made possible through a generous donation, the laboratory is housed in the recently-constructed Eric and Sarah Rodgers Science and Engineering Library, about two blocks from the main library building. As presently equipped, the lab consists of two workstations. One workstation is designed for those with limited vision-that is, for those who need material (text or graphics) enlarged. Through Telesensory cards and software, the workstation links a personal computer to a large-screen VGA monitor as well as to a Closed Circuit Display (CCD) camera and a separate video/TV monitor. Access routs are also available to a laser printer and a Telesensory Everest Braille Embosser. It is .also possible to use Vert Pro, a text-to-voice synthesizer. Most important of all, users are able to access AMELIA (the Libraries' online catalog) and the Internet and have information enlarged or "read" to them. In certain instances, two users can work simultaneously at the workstation, one using the CCD system and the other the online catalog or a word processor.

The second workstation is for use primarily by persons who are unable to read at all. It is equipped with a personal computer and super VGA monitor, the Vert speech recognition system, and the OsCar optical character recognition system. The OsCar enables text to be scanned and projected on to the monitor and either ready by the voice synthesizer or stored for later use. The material can be converted to a word processing programme and edited, or printed on a laser printer or the Everest Braille Embosser. This workstation also allows access to AMELIA and the Internet as well to the other options available on the Rodgers Library LAN.

Installation of and initial training for the adaptive equipment was provided by representatives from

Telesensory, the primary vendor. After this phase, the chair of the electronic access subcommittee of the University Libraries Committee on Specialized Access (a library staff member with computer expertise) assumed responsibility for equipment and training. It was expected that committee members (including the blind and visually impaired students who were the lab's first users) would train the next generation. The opening of the lab was accompanied by a massive public relations campaign, including press and television coverage and a series of demonstrations for alumni and townspeople as well as the traditional student population. These quickly developed a user clientele. Yet more important than sheer hours of use is quality of use. Within months, several users were working independently in the lab who previously would have required readers and constant direct assistance.

But marvelous as adaptive equipment is, there are a surprising number of library transactions that must be handled the old-fashioned way-through direct personal assistance. Users with visual impairments still need research and reference assistance with print sources that are too cumbersome to transport to the adaptive lab or too difficult to use without help; even the use of an index can be excruciatingly complex for the visually disabled. They also need help with electronic sources that are not available in adaptive formats (CD-ROMs on stand-alone stations for example). Standard reference procedures need to be rethought, and sometimes become as complex and time-consuming to the librarians as to the patron. A user cannot be told to browse the southern history collection for the perfect source on the civil war or that the encyclopedias are "by the window." Once a source has been found, a user without sight may be unable to photocopy the needed pages to be used on adaptive equipment or given to readers. And assistance is particularly needed if a user finds a citation in an index to a source available only in microform. Beyond reference, the standard bibliographic instruction programme of a tour with handouts may be impossible.

In the early stages of the Libraries' work with the visually impaired, most library assistance to disabled users was handled through the reference unit, a result of the circumstance that the chair of the Libraries Committee on Specialized Access (who soon became the Coordinator for Services to Library Users with Disabilities) was a reference librarian.

Other reference staff members and student workers assisted with all library needs-paging and photocopying as well as research. The burden soon became more than the reference staff alone could handle; gradually the users were weaned from the reference unit and encouraged to take their needs directly to other appropriate departments. This was not always easily done. Like others, disabled patrons were comfortable working with staff members who had helped them successfully in the past. Today, new users are asked to contact departments directly for routine assistance, and the entire library staff is encouraged to handle all but the most complex requests.

A policy statement prepared by committee members provides guidance to staff. Users are encouraged to plan ahead to allow the staff time to provide special assistance. Meeting the needs of individuals with other disabilities has been easier and more straightforward. Persons with hearing impairments conduct most business at the Libraries without difficulty (although emergency evacuation for the hearing impaired remains a pressing concern). To enable the hearing impaired to receive telephone reference assistance and to conduct other library transactions by telephone, the libraries have acquired a TDD (telecommunications device for the deaf).

The TDD enables the Libraries' staff to receive and send typed messages over telephone lines to a hearing impaired person with another TDD. The Libraries also participate in the Alabama Relay Network, itself part of a national network service of intermediaries that transact telephone business for the hearing impaired. A recent and representative transaction consisted of a TDD patron keyboarding a request for a book to a TDD operator at the network, who called the reference desk to check if the libraries held the book in question. The libraries did not-it was a cookbook-and the reply was returned in TDD form via the network operator. At present, no user has requested a signer or bibliographic instruction tour with an interpreter; the Libraries would enlist the services of the Disabled-Student Services if one became necessary.

Libraries offering adult and children's programmes or video collections probably will find it useful to train a staff member to sign and provide equipment with closed-caption decoding capabilities; by law most television sets currently on the market have built-in closed caption capability. Persons with mobility impairments constitute a large portion of the disabled user population. The Libraries have found that most are able to take care of their own library needs. All buildings in the system are wheelchair-accessible, have specially designated parking spaces and curb cuts, and are equipped with wheelchair-accessible AMELIA and CD-ROM terminals. Elevators are presently being fitted with protruding buttons for users with poor hand coordination. At present, the main concerns of library users with motor impairments are navigating the stacks and retrieving items from high shelves or hard-to-access areas-a retired stack collection housed in the basement, for example. However, the expanded use of very large, motorized carts and wheelchairs has increased rather than decreased mobility problems in tight or confined spaces-individuals using these devices have considerable difficulty entering elevators and using photocopying, microform, and terminal equipment. Like users with visual impairments, these users are encouraged to let the staff in each department know what they need and, if possible, to give advance notice. The Libraries' renewed commitment to provide full services for persons with disabilities has led to the development of staff awareness and publicity programmes. The staff awareness programme is designed to introduce the staff to the library needs of users with disabilities and to reinforce the Libraries' commitment to these users. The programme is also a sensitivity awareness programme for, as Zipkowitz points out, some staff members are not eager to serve all populations.

In one instance at the Libraries, a staff member was unwilling to assist a person who was not visibly disabled-in this case an arthritic person. Particularly difficult situations arise with users whose disabilities make their behaviour unusual or difficult, as is sometimes the case with some kinds of mental and learning disabilities, or with disfigured users. The staff awareness programme addresses these very hard issues.

The Libraries have had to train student workers, for example, to work with a user who, for reasons of physical disability, virtually screams. A central part of the staff awareness programme is a manual prepared by the staff awareness subcommittee, sent to every staff member for personal use and used in a disability awareness segment of the Libraries' new staff orientation programme.

The manual offers suggestions for assisting users with visual, hearing, mobility, developmental and learning disabilities. In addition, it contains a list of persons on campus who work with the disabled, and some general information on the ADA. Student workers, often the first staff members library users encounter, also will be trained in serving the disabled through a segment conducted by the Coordinator during the yearly student worker orientation workshops. A strong public relations campaign has brought the Libraries' efforts to the attention of the campus and the local community. An effective part of the campaign has been demonstrations of the adaptive equipment by blind and visually impaired students for alumni, University administration, and interested community and campus groups.

A highpoint of the public relations effort was the inauguration of the adaptive lab, during which guests from around the state and the local media had a chance to view the equipment and to talk to students about their use of the lab and their other library needs. As a result of the publicity generated by the inauguration, the School of Communications at the University prepared a short programme on the adaptive lab, which was aired on Alabama Public Television. Recently, a local television network filmed a graduate student who has cerebral palsy using the wheel-chair--accessible AMELIA and CD-ROM terminals, and being helped at the circulation desk.

The film was shown on the local United Cerebral Palsy Telephone and is being considered for the 1995 national telephone. The Libraries began to develop the programme for services to users with disabilities with a great deal of enthusiasm, confident that the problems that invariably arise with any new endeavour would be easily worked through. Yet the Libraries were working with a new group of users with complex and very individual needs as well as with new technologies and new and extremely vague legislation.

Launching the programme proved slower than anticipated; satisfactory solutions to some problems are still being sought, and new problems keep cropping up. Some services, bibliographic instruction for example, have not yet been standardized and are being handled on an individual basis. Many of the continuing concerns centre on the adaptive lab. The installation of equipment was a long and difficult process. An initial specification proved inadequate, and the Libraries were forced to oarder new equipment, notably a personal computer with a more powerful microprocessor and significantly more RAM. The vendor was repeatedly called upon to provide additional training; considerable assistance was also sought from campus computer experts. Once up and running, both workstations experienced system failures from unknown causes, leaving users and staff frustrated.

The training of new users, at first handled by members of the electronic access subcommittee, bogged down as it became apparent that some adaptive equipment was difficult to use and some users had impairments that made training complex; training required anywhere from ten minutes to ten hours, depending on the computer skills and particular needs of the user. Subcommittee members, with regular library jobs or classes to attend, were unable to afford the time proper training required.

Clearly too much was asked of the student committee members, who had quite enough to do managing their own affairs. And as publicity attracted new users, management of the lab became an additional concern. Located in a second floor room of a branch library, access to the lab and equipment was hard to monitor. Yet access had to be controlled: expensive equipment had to be protected from accidents and unintentional abuse as well as from theft. Students also used the lab's equipment for appropriate but originally unanticipated purposes. While the lab was originally designed to meet users' needs for library access, students delighted with the capabilities of the equipment used the lab for a variety of homework needs. The equipment was not always available for AMELIA use or to "read" library materials, and walk-ins sometimes had lengthy waits.

The lab's success also created a need for more management and attention than the committee could give. Recently, a decision was made to focus the committee effort more on advocacy and to put the actual management, training, and equipment maintenance in the hands of the staff members of the Rodgers Library, the ADA Coordinator, and a computer consultant. At present, all staff members at the Rodges Library are being trained to assist users in scanning and enlarging material and accessing AMELIA.

Simple user guides are being prepared and will soon be available in Braille and enlarged formats. More extensive training will be handled through the Coordinator with guidance from the consultant and Disabled-Student Services. Institutional arrangements have also needed refining. Since not only the Libraries are involved in ADA activities, continuing efforts are needed to identify and coordinate adaptive computer services on campus. Library staff members are part of a University committee devoted this task.

This group will attempt to determine what adaptive equipment should be available on campus and who should be responsible for training, maintenance, and publicity. Ideally, adaptive equipment will be more widely available in campus computer labs for homework needs, and the library lab will be primarily used for library tasks.

The generous gift that established the lab was blessing, and so it remains. Because of it, the Libraries had a high-profile, relatively quick "result" to display-a great benefit to its users, a morale-builder for individual staff, an encouragement to other donors. But the lab also put us on the high seas of ADA technology and administration before we had learned to swim, or even had our life vests. Again, had the Libraries the benefit of experience-even other's experience-we would have avoided at least some of our errors. We would not have underestimated training needs and would have understood the wisdom of buying hardware seemingly in excess of current needs.

Of course, not all experience is transferable. As Dalton points out in her "Exemplary Library Programmes and Services for Those With Disabilities" in *The Americans with Disabilities Act: Its Impact on Libraries The Library's Responses in "Double" Steps*, there are many different ways to provide services to the disabled. The committee approach, and the equipment and services chosen by the University of Alabama Libraries may not be appropriate for a different user population, or a library with different funding and staffing arrangements. The University of Alabama Libraries chose adaptive equipment, as the most appropriate choice for a large university library attempting to meet the needs of an academically diverse population ranging from freshman to doctoral candidates. A community library with a different user population may prefer to emphasize a large print, Braille, or talking book collection or to offer a volunteer reader service. A library may find that a delivery programme for users unable to leave their homes is a necessary part of its services or that a resource center would best suit the needs of its users.

There is no single right way. The needs of a particular community will become apparent with an evaluation of users and current services. Fortunately, the growing literature and electronic resources now ensure that libraries need not work alone in determining a suitable programme. While the Libraries will continue to work on publicity and staff awareness programmes and to refine the management of the lab, future efforts will focus more on institutional cooperation, funding for additional labs, and unresolved issues connected with adequate emergency procedures for persons with disabilities. Bolstered by success but slightly more hesitant and certainly wiser because of setbacks, the Libraries face these challenges acutely aware that efforts to meet the needs of the disabled, like the lives of the disabled themselves, will never be a matter entirely of routine.

REFERENCES

A. J. Cropley, *Lifelong Education: a Psychological Analysis* (New York: Pergamon, 1977), pp. 57-58, Wills W. Harman, "Recent Psychological and Psychic Research: Implications for Science and Society," *in The Future of Education: Policy Issues and Challenge,* ed. Kathryn Cirincione-Coles (Beverly Hills: Sage, 1981), p. 218.

and Other Service Professionals (Phoenix: Oryx Press, 1990).

Anita S. Harbert and Leon H. Ginsberg, *Human Services for Older Adults: Concepts and Skills,* 2nd revised (Columbia, SC: University of South Carolina Press, 1990): 3,54-80.

Barbara T. Mates, *Library Technology for Visually and Physically Impaired Patrons,* (Westport: Meckler, 1991).

Betty J. Turock, "Public Library Service for Older Adults: Update 1984, "*Library Quarterly* 57 (April 1987): 143.

Betty J. Turock, *Information and Aging* (Jefferson, NC.: McFarland, 1988), p. 1.

Betty J. Turock, *Serving the Older Adult: a Guide to Library Programmes and Information Sources* (New York: Bowker, 1982); Genevieve M. Casey, *Library Services for the Aging* (Hamden, CT: Library Professional Publications, 1984).

Casey, *Library Services for the Aging, p. 7*

Christopher G. Lewis, "The Americans with Disabilities Act and its Effect on Public Libraries, "*Public Libraries 31* (January/ February 1992): 23-8.

Christopher W. Nolan, "Closing the Reference Interview: Implications for Policy and Practice, " RQ 31 (Summer 1992): 513-523.

Connie Van Fleet, "Lifelong Learning Theory and the Provision of Adult Services" *in Adult Services: an Enduring Focus for Public Libraries,* ed. Kathleen M. Heim and Danny P. Wallace (Chicago: ALA, 1990), pp. 166-265.

Darlene E. Weingand, "The Invisible Client: Meeting the Needs of Persons With Learning Disabilities," *The Reference Librarian 31* (1990): 77-88.

Denise Perry Donavin, *Aging with Style and Savvy* (Chcago: ALA, 1990), p. 27, reporting on *Love, Sex, and Aging: a Consumers Union Report,* Edward M. Brecher and the Editors of Consumer Reports Books (PLACE, Little, Brown, 1984).

Don Fersh and Peter W. Thomas, *Complying with the Americans with Disabilities Act: a Guidebook for Management and People with Disabilities* (West-port: Quorum Books, 1993).

Elaine Landau, "The Challenge of Film Programming for Older Adults, "*The Bookmark* 42 (Winter 1984): 102.

Elinor B. Waters and Jane Goodman, Empowering *Older Adults: Practical Strategies for Counselors* (San Francisco: Jossey-Bass Publishers, 1990): p. xi.

Elizabeth Vierck, Fact Book on Aging (Santa Barbara, CA: ABC-CLIO, 1990): 3.

J. B. Black et. al., *Surveying Public Libraries for the* ADA. (Pinellas County, Florida: Pinellas Public Library Cooperative, 1992).

J. Roby Kidd, *How Adults Learn* (New York: Association Press, 1959), p. 90; K. A. McClelland, "Self-conception and Life

Satisfaction: Integrating Aged Subculture and Activity Theory, "*Journal of Gerontoglogy* 37 (1982): 723.

Joanne L. Crispin, ed., *The Americans with Disabilities Act. Its Impact on Libraries The Library's Responses in "Doable" Steps,*·(Chicago: American Library Association, 1993).

John J. Jax and Theresa Muraski, "Library Services for Students with Disabilities at the University of Wisconsin-Stout, "*The Journal of Academic Librarianship* 19 (July 1993): 166-68.

Joyce G. Saricks and Nancy Brown, *Reader's Advisory Service in the Public Library* (Chicago: ALA, 1989).

Keith C. Wright and Judith F. Davie, *Serving the Disabled* (New York: Neal-Schuman Publishers, 1991).

Library Trends 41 (Summer 1992) Libraries Serving an Underserved Population: Deaf and Hearing-Impaired Patrons.

Lowrence O. Gostin and Henry A. Beyer, eds., *Implementing the Americans with Disabilities Act: Rights and Responsibilities of all Americans (*Baltimore: P. H. Brookes Pub. Co., 1993).

Mary Jo Brazil, *Building Library Collections on Aging: a Selection Guide and Core List* (Santa Barbara, CA: ABC-CLIO,1990); Rhea J. Rubin and Gail McGovern, *Working with older Adults: A Handbook for Libraries, 2nd* (Sacaramento, CA: California State Library, 1988); Elizabeth A. Hudson, *Libraries for a Lifetime* (Oklahoma City: The Oklahoma Department of Libraries, 1989).

Melanie J. Norton, "Effective Bibliographic Instruction for Deaf and Hearing-Impaired College Students, "*Library Trends 41 (*Summer 1992): 118-50.

Michael G. Gunde, "Libraries and the Americans with Disabilities Act, " pp. 1-31 and Ruth O'Donnel, "Planning to Implement the ADA in the Library," pp. 32-70 in Donald D. Foos and Nancy C. Pack, eds., *How Libraries Must Comply with the Americans with Disabilities Act.* (ADA) (Phoenix: Oryx Press, 1992).

Patrick Penland, "Adult Self-Planned Learning," *Public Libraries* 17 (Summer 1978): 6-8; Allen Tough, *The Adults Learning Projects: a Fresh Approach to Theory and Practice in Adult Learning, 2nd ed. (*Austin, TX: Learning Concepts, 1979);

Malcolm S. Knowles, *The Modern Practice of Adult Education*, revised and updated (Chicago: Association Press, 1980).

Paula Brown Doress and Diana Laskin Siegal, *Ourselves, Growing Older: Women Aging with Knowledge and Power* (New York: Touchstone, 1987).

Phyllis Dalton, "Exemplary Library Programmes and Services for Those with Disabilities," 27-33 in Joanne L. Crispin, *The American with Disabilities Act.*

Ruth A Velleman, *Meeting the Needs of People*

Waters and Goodman; Anne M. Ring, Read Easy: *large Print Libraries for Older Adults* (Seattle: CARE source Programme Development, Inc.: 1991).

With Disabilities: a Guide for Librarians, Educators,

Zipkowits, "No One Wants to See Them'," 54-5.

4

Reference Sources

> "Disappointment to a noble soul is what cold water is to burning metal: it strengthens-tempers, intensifies, but never destroys it.
>
> —*Eliza Tabor*

First, it is pertinent to note that success in doing research is largely a matter of combining knowledge of techniques, knowledge of sources and persistence. Researchers initiating inquiries will want to be aware of specialized encyclopaedias and state-of-the-art review articles and then of the several techniques that can be used to find more in-depth information:

1. Controlled vocabulary subject heading searches in manual indexes.
2. Systematic browsing.
3. Key word searches in manual indexes.
4. Citation searches in manual indexes.
5. Searches using published bibliographies.
6. Computer searches (which can be done via subject headings, key words, or citations, but add the possibility [among other advantages] of post-coordinate Boolean combinations while [among other

limitations] diminishing the possibilities of browsing).

7. Talking to knowledgeable people.

Remarkably, each of these seven methods is potentially applicable in any subject area; each has distinct advantages and disadvantages; and each is capable of turning up information that cannot be reached by the other six. It is also advisable to remember that all computer searches have noteworthy limitations, that Boolean combinations of subjects can be accomplished by both online and noncomputer methods and that particular treasures lie in special collections, government documents and microform collections—which must be sought out more actively than other sources. A knowledge of these few distinct techniques—and of the advantages and limitations of each—will enable most researchers to substantially increase the range and efficiency of their investigations in any subject area. Most scholars, unfortunately, do most of their research only on the basis of (1) looking at footnotes in sources they already have, (2) inefficient use of card catalogues and (3) general browsing in the classified bookstacks of libraries. Those in the sciences tend to minimize even these pursuits, relying instead on taking to acquaintances.

Very few researchers use catalogues and indexes efficiently because they routinely look under the wrong terms (confusing titles with subject headings or looking under generic rather than specific headings) and because they are familiar with only a small fraction of the range of indexes that exist.

Reference to the outline of procedures sketched above, however, will enable most researchers to gain a simple overview of the *full range of options* available to them in any inquiry and also assist them to achieve a sense of "closure" in making estimates of what research remains to be done.

Basically, a A knowledge of techniques, however, must be supplemented by a knowledge of sources. And this is facilitated by an understanding that the finding aids and reference materials in any field predictably tend to fall into certain *types* of publications that collectively form a kind of structure within the literature. ("Reference materials" means those that either point the way into the core literature contained in journals, reports, monographs, dissertations, etc.; or those that summarize, abstract, digest, or review it. Reference materials tend to be those forms of literature that are simply consulted rather than read from cover to cover). A foreknowledge of this overall structure can alert you to distribute your efforts among a variety of paths of inquiry; it can also give you a sense of what further options are available if your initial attempts are unsuccessful in finding the desired information.

The various "bones" within the reference structure are:

1. *Indexes and abstracts.* These serve to get you to the journal articles and research reports on your subject. Abstracts have the added advantage of providing brief summaries of the items they index, which enable you to do a quick literature review at an early stage of your research.
2. *Encyclopaedias.* Here the specialized sets devoted to particular subject areas are often more useful than the widely known general sets. The purpose of an encyclopaedia is to summarize knowledge and to provide a starting point for more extensive

research; it seeks to present an overview of a subject written in such a way that a nonspecialist can understand it. (Note that sets specialized in a particular *subject area* still tend to be written with a nonspecialist *audience* in mind). An encyclopaedia may be contrasted to a *treatise,* which attempts to provide all knowledge on a subject in a systematic (rather than an alphabetical) arrangement and which may be written for specialists rather than laypeople.

3. *Computer databases.* These often contain the same information as conventional indexes and abstracts, but they offer the advantage of allowing you to comb through it in different ways (*e.g.*, by key word searches and post-coordinate Boolean combinations).
4. *Handbooks and Almanacs.* These serve as compendia of a variety of miscellaneous information and are often especially good for tabular or statistical data.
5. *Bibliographies.* These list publications on a particular subject, often including materials that are missed by online databases.
6. *Guides to the literature.* These often provide a connected expository overview of the literature of a subject and its reference sources.
7. *Review articles.* State-of-the-art reviews are somewhat like encyclopaedia articles in attempting to provide an overall assessment of the state of knowledge of a particular subject. They are often longer, however; they are frequently written for an audience of specialists familiar with a particular jargon; and they often seek to provide comprehensive rather than simply introductory bibliographies.
8. *Directories.* These serve to lead you to people,

organizations, or institutions that are interested in and knowledgeable about particular subjects. They are especially valuable because they often provide the best key to the tremendous stores of knowledge that exist outside libraries.

9. *Yearbooks.* These provide reviews and assessments of the most recent year's developments in a field.
10. *Newsletters and loose-leaf services.* These provide daily or weekly updates of information in rapidly changing fields.

Within several of these categories it is useful to distinguish further which sources are searchable by subject headings, by key words, or by classified subject-grouping arrangement. The *method* of searching involved will have a significant effect on the results that can be achieved. Students within a particular discipline usually learn its reference sources from a particular list they are given to study. The result is that they often learn the individual trees very well without perceiving the arrangement of the forest or the variety of methods available for getting through it, whether by walking, riding, flying over, swinging from branch to branch, or burrowing underneath. The training of reference librarians, on the other hand, is more from the top down than from the bottom up. They learn first the overall arrangement that can be expected in *any* forest—here the analogy is not perfect—and the various methods of moving around in it.

They hold an overall set of *categories* of sources in mind, with a knowledge of several distinct methods of combing each category (*e.g.*, "What this question requires is a bibliography arranged by a subject classification scheme rather than alphabetically by subject headings"; "What this question demands is an index that allows a key word approach rather than subject heading access"; "What this question requires is a database that allows citation searching coupled with post-coordinate limitations by key words").

Even though they may not know particular titles or file names within a subject area, they do know beforehand that they can *reasonably expect* to find certain *types* of sources within which they can *reasonably expect* to find certain *methods* of access available, each with its own advantages and disadvantages. They therefore usually understand the *full range of options* for finding information even on unfamiliar subjects; for this reason they can often provide material on a subject more efficiently than even full professors within the discipline.

The librarians may not understand the content of the discipline; but they do understand the predictable systems and methods of *finding* the content, which is a distinct matter. And the study of what can be expected in the arrangement, categorization, storage and retrieval of information is a discipline unto itself: it is called library and information science. Those who have not studied it formally should be very careful about assuming that they are doing fully efficient research "on their own", for there will almost always be more options in searching than they realize.

The moral of the story is brief: the more you know of what your options are, the better the searcher you will be; but remember to ask for help because the probability is that you will miss something important if you work entirely on your own.

Librarians have three major aids that help them to exploit the internal structure of the information sources within any given field. The first can be considered the basic source; the other two, updates. These include:

1. *Guide to Reference Books,* edited by Eugene Sheehy (10th ed.; American Library Association, 1986). This volume, known as "Sheehy", is the reference librarian's bible. It enables a searcher to look up any subject field and find within it a definitive listing of virtually all its important reference sources arranged according to the types of literature. The citations provide full bibliographic descriptions of each source for exact identification, plus descriptive annotations. The overall arrangement of the volume is by broad subject groups, with an index by authors, title and subjects.

2. *Reference Sources* (Pierian Press, 1977). This annual publication is a comprehensive list of reference sources in all fields published during the year. Beginning with the 1980 volume it is arranged alphabetically by LC subject headings, with indexes by author and title. It is most useful as an ongoing and regular update of the latest Sheehy edition.

3. *ARBA: American Reference Books Annual,* edited by Bohdan S. Wynar (Libraries Unlimited, Inc., 1970). Each annual volume in this series presents a listing of all reference books published in the United States within the preceding year. The distinctive feature of the series is that it provides a detailed review of each work listed. Indexes are by author, title and subject. *ARBA* thus serves as another excellent update of Sheehy. Three five-year cumulative indexes (1970-1974, 1975-1979

> and 1980-1984) have appeared since the beginning of the series and these cumulations are themselves major guides to reference books. Some libraries keep them next to their Sheehy.

Notably, there is still another volume—a kind of "mini-Sheehy" —that every researcher should own. This is *Reference Books: A Brief Guide,* compiled by Marion V. Bell and Eleanor A. Swidan (Enoch Pratt Free Library, revised irregularly). It is an excellent brief list, with comparative and evaluative annotations, of the most important reference sources in all fields. Ordering information can be found in *Paperbound Books in Print.*

5

Circulation Services

> "No horse gets anywhere until he is harrased. No steam power drives anything until it is confined. No Niagra is ever turned into light and power until it is focused, dedicated and disciplined.
>
> —***Harry Emerson Fosdik***

Now we turn to circulation system which is an important function of libraries.

First we will touch circulation control system and then proceed to issue of patron registration.

Circulation Control System

Charging out materials from the library is a primary function of public services. For many patrons the only direct contact with the library is at the circulation point where materials are charged out. It is essential, therefore, that circulation department staff be aware of the need for good public relations.

The library's circulation control system should be easy to use, since a cumbersome or complex system can be an obstacle to good service. To provide the best service, all circulation staff must understand the circulation control system. The reason for circulating materials out of the library is to allow the borrower the convenience of using materials whenever and wherever is desirable. Most libraries, however, have certain materials that are not allowed to circulate, or that have only limited circulation. This may be because of the rarity, the value, or the format of the materials; for example, non-circulating items might include rare books, reference materials, or reels of microfilm.

Charging out materials is only "the tip of the iceberg" of all the work performed by a circulation department. Other duties may include discharging (checking in) materials, overdue and fine work, reserve book control, shelving, general shelf maintenance, shelf reading, shifting materials, inventory control, and interlibrary loan.

Selection

In fact, selecting a circulation control system is one of the first decisions made when establishing a library. The system selected must be coordinated with processing of materials for use. Before material can be made ready for use, it must be known whether the circulation control system will require a book pocket and book card, a date due slip, a punched card, or a bar code.

The method of circulating books affects other library operations. Careful study is needed to select a circulation system, because once it is operating any change or major modification will be costly and time-consuming. Many considerations are involved in the selection of a circulation control system.

The first is the size of the library collection and the expected volume of circulation. Some systems, well suited to a small volume of circulation, would be inadequate in a larger library. And, of course, the opposite is also true: an automated system may be needed in a library circulating

500,000 items a year, but may be unnecessary in a library circulating 50,000 items a year.

A second factor is the cost of the system. Three elements are involved here: (1) the initial cost of processing and equipment; (2) the cost of ongoing processing, equipment maintenance, and supplies; and (3) the cost of personnel needed to operate the system. This kind of analysis is complex and requires detailed research. A carefully selected circulation system may save many thousands of dollars each year.

Further a third factor is the type of patron the library will serve..The basic decision here is the kind and amount of borrower participation built into the system. Some systems require that the borrower merely hand the material to library personnel, who do everything necessary to charge it out. Other systems require that the borrower fill out cards with the author and title of the item, the borrower's name, and his identification number. In a public library, where patrons range from the semi-literate to the university graduate, the circulation control system must accommodate a wide range of abilities.

To avoid errors in borrower participation, a public library might use a system in which the patron hands over the material and the library personnel do the actual charging out. At the other end of the spectrum is the academic or special library. Since it serves a select clientele from whom relatively error-free participation can be expected, the library may save personnel by letting the patron do as much as possible.

A last and fourth consideration is the quality of service given to the patron. To some degree all of the preceding factors must be balanced with the library's standards of what constitutes good service. The circulation control system must be compatible with the needs of the library's users and the overall purpose of the library.

Main Characteristics

A circulation control system has unique characte-ristics that determine its value to a library. The characteristics discussed below are found, in varying degrees, in all systems. When a system is being selected, the importance of each characteristic for a library's operation must be considered. First, the system must be easy for the patrons to use and for library personnel to operate. A complex or cumbersome system may result in poor service and poor public relations if the patron views it as an obstacle to his needs rather than as an aid.

Simplicity and ease of use might be the most important quality of any circulation control system. Second, the system should allow the library to identify the borrower, the material borrowed, and the date material is due to be returned. All systems can provide this information, but vary in the speed with which it can be retrieved.

In some libraries this information may not be needed instantly. In academic libraries, however, one requirement might be that the borrower's name and the due date of materials charged out must be available immediately. Third, the system should provide a record of overdue materials. This information is needed for sending overdue notices, for providing a record for fines, and for developing a list of materials for possible replacement.

All circulation systems can provide this information, but they vary in the speed with which the information can be retrieved. Some libraries must identify overdue material daily, while other libraries need to do it less often. Fourth, the system should provide easy and accurate retrieval of reserved materials when they are checked in. Patrons often request materials already out on loan. The patron should be able to leave a request to be notified when material is returned and available for further use. The request is called a "reserve" or "hold" request.

At some point the system must allow for returned materials to be checked against reserve requests and held for the next borrower. Reserve work is an important service; when it is well run, it can be a good public relations tool.

Finally, the system should allow easy retrieval of statistics required by the library. For some libraries a manual system provides sufficient statistics with minimal effort. Other libraries my need sophisticated statistics on reading patterns or collection-use requiring a computerized system.

It is remarkable that about 30 different circulation control systems are currently used in American libraries. Most of them, however, are not widely used. Four systems are now in general use. They are: (1) Newark system, (2) Gaylord system, (3) Photographic systems, and (4) Automated computer-based system. Our discussion will be limited to general description of these systems.

Further, reader should remember that each library has special needs and may alter a circulation system to meet those needs. Even libraries using the same system may have variations in operating details. For this reason the following descriptions are general and do not cover operating details.

As with so many library functions, the best way to learn is through practical work experience under the guidance of an experienced LMTA or librarian. The reader would benefit from visiting libraries to see various systems in operation.

Newark System

The Newark circulation control system is the most widely used system in the United States. It is simple to use for patrons and staff and is suitable for both small and medium-sized libraries. The system requires no expensive equipment. There are two variations of the system: (1) "self-charge," which requires borrower participation, and (2) "staff-charge," with no borrower participation. When the "self-charge," method is used, the borrower removes the book card from the book pocket and writes name, identification number, or other required information on the first available blank line. The borrower gives the book and book card to the library clerk, who stamps the due date in the book and on the book card. At this time the borrower may be asked to show a library registration card or some other form of identification. The book card is then ready to be filed by due date and call number or only by call number.

One variation files book cards by author instead of call number. In this case it is necessary to have the call number, author's name, and title on the book card and book pocket. This is an example of how the method of processing material in technical services is determined by the circulation system.

The "staff-charge" method requires a library staff member, not the borrower to fill out the information on the book card. The borrower gives the clerk the material to be charged out and his or her library card. In this method each library card has an identification number, and this number is placed on the book card instead of the borrower's name. The staff member would not sign the patron's name; the patron could later claim the signature was forged. The remaining steps are the same as in the "self-charge" method. "Self-charge" is more expensive to operate because of increased staff time, but it should reduce the number of errors. When material is returned, the book card is removed from the file. This ends the borrower's responsibility. The book card is placed back into the book pocket, and the material is ready for circulation.

Gaylord System

Notably, this circulation control system is named for the manufacture of the electric book charger used in charging out materials. It is similar to the Newark system except that a machine is used to fill in the information on the book card, which frees both the borrower and library personnel from this time-consuming task. This system requires no borrower participation. When the borrower registers with the library, he or she is given a library identification card with an identification number embossed on a metal plate.

One variation of the charging machine allows the use of a plastic identification card, which can print directly on the book card. If the identification card with the embossed plate is used, registration files of borrowers by name and identi-fication number will be needed, since only the identification number appears on the book card (Figs. 3.4 and 3.5). With the plastic identification card, the borrower's name can be printed on the book card eliminating the need for a registration file by identification number. To charge out material the borrower presents the material and identification card to the attendant. The book card is removed from the book pocket and inserted into a slot in the charging machine.

The identification card is inserted into another slot and the machine automatically prints the information—borrower's name or identification number and a due date—on the book card.

Then a predated date due card is placed in the book pocket. The book card is now ready to be filed by due date and in order by call number or author. Material is discharged by removing the book card from the file and placing it back into the book pocket. When the date due card is removed from the pocket, the material is ready for reshelving.

Photographic Charging

This type of circulation control system is characterized by the use of a camera to photograph each transaction on microfilm and the use of a transaction number to identify it. Many different companies manufacture equipment for this types of circulation control system, and each piece of equipment may have a unique quality suitable to a particular library. Below is a general description of photographic charging.

The reader must realize that the details of operating the systems will vary with the equipment used and with the requirements of a library The borrower presents the material to be charged out, along with an identification card, to the attendant. In this circulation control system the identification must carry the borrower's name, but it will not necessarily be a library card. The identification could be a driver's license or some other kind of identification. The material is placed under the camera with the book pocket in position to be photographed.

Then the borrower's identification and the dated and numbered date due card—the transaction slip with the transaction number—are placed on the machine in position to be photographed. The photograph will include all the information needed to identify the material, the borrower's name, and the due date. If the author, title, and call number are not on the book pocket, a book card with this information will be necessary.

To complete the charging-out procedure, the attendant inserts the dated transaction slip into the book pocket. Material is discharged when transaction slip is removed from the book pocket.

In a library with high circulation, it may not be feasible to use a serial-number sheet. In this situation it is possible to have the transaction number keypunched into the transaction slip. When the material is returned the keypunched transaction slips are sent to a computer center. The computer can be programmed to print out lists of transaction numbers for materials not returned.

These are several methods of checking which material has been returned and which overdue. One way is to use a serial-number sheet. The attendant checks the due date on the transaction slip and matches it with the corresponding due date on the serial-number sheet. As material is discharged the transaction slip number is crossed off the serial-number sheet. After a time the numbers not crossed off will be considered overdue. The microfilm record—in sequence by transaction number—can be checked for the borrower's name so that overdue procedures can be started.

Automated Circulation Control

It is worth mentioning that the newest circulation systems are computerized systems. If the LMTA were to make assumptions based on the number of articles, seminars, and professional discussions about automated circulation, he or she might conclude that every library was automated! This is not true. In 1983 probably less than 1,000 libraries in the United States had operating automated circulated systems. This is less than 5% of all libraries.

Two factors have been primarily responsible for the low number of operating systems: (1) Relatively high costs to purchase a system for a small or medium-sized library. In 1980 the average cost was $100,000 plus any required building modifications. And, (2) To be cost effective a library needs approximately 400,000 or more transactions annually. Manual systems usually work well with less than 400,000 transactions. The latest developments in microcomputers coupled with lower cost for hardware, however, may mean more affordable systems will be widely available in the next few years.

Computer circulation systems require little or no patron participation. Each library user is assigned a unique identification number that appears as a bar-encoded number (also called zebra number) that can be read by a light pen or a laser scanner. Anyone who shops in a grocery store will recognize the bar-codes, which are similar to those that appear on most grocery items. Similarly each item in the library's collection is also given a unique bar-code.

These requirements will affect technical processing procedures when materials are prepared for use; and they will affect registration procedures. To charge out an item the patron presents a special identification card with the bar-code and the material to be charged out to the attendant at the circulation desk. The clerk "reads" the bar-code on the identification card with a light pen or with a laser scanner. The computer automatically checks the patron's status to see if he or she is eligible to borrow materials (i.e., no current excessive overdue fines, currently enrolled in school, etc.). If the patron's status report is satisfactory, the clerk "reads" the bar-code on each item to be charged out.

The information about the patron and each item charged to the patron is now recorded in the computer's memory. The identification card is returned and the transaction is completed. To check in returned material the light pen or scanner is placed in a discharge mode. When the bar-code on the item is "read" it automatically clears the record from the computer's memory.

The patron's record is cleared and his or her responsibility ends. If another patron has a reserve (hold) on the item this is indicated on the CRT (cathode ray tube) terminal and the clerk can take appropriate action. Some systems allow information to be entered by a keyboard terminal with a CRT to display information. At least one system has a portable unit with an independent power source that allows materials to be charged out at remote locations such as on a bookmobile, or that can be used during a power failure.

In fact, computer-based systems also allow multibranch library systems or cooperating independent libraries to communicate circulation and library collection information to each other using ordinary telephone lines. This is a valuable enhancement of service and is especially useful for interlibrary loans.

Below is a list of tasks most computer systems can be programmed to perform. Each of these tasks is labour intensive and costly in a manual system. If these tasks can be performed by a computer a library can improve service and, perhaps, even save money:

(1) Identifies delinquent borrowers who have overdue material or owe fines or both.

(2) Displays the reason for the delinquency.

(3) Alerts staff to lost or stolen identification cards when one is presented.

(4) Indicates when a reserve(hold) has been placed on an item.

(5) Displays all items checked out to a borrower.

(6) Allows placement and cancellation of reserves (holds).

(7) Calculates fines and fees for overdue items.

(8) Automatically prints recall notices.

(9) Automatically prints fee statements.

(10) Indicates whether a particular item is already checked out or is temporarily unavailable—i.e., at the bindery.

(11) Records a variety of statistical information concerning collection use and circulation activities.

Because these systems are so flexible a library can tailor the functions cited above meet its specific needs. The only way to really understand an automated circulation system is to see one in operation. A visit to a successful operating system is far more useful than just reading a description.

Non-book Materials

Notably, the circulation control systems we have described are capable of handling all kinds of library materials, nonetheless many libraries choose to handle certain non-book materials separately. This, however, does not tend to be true in libraries with automated circulation.

Borrower participation is usually required. Also, the loan periods for these materials may be different from those for books. Libraries develop their own special forms for charging out non-book material. To charge out such materials the borrower fills out a special charge card for whatever kind of material is involved.

While it may be possible to use the same circulation control system for both special materials and books, many libraries choose not to do so. The cost of controlling these special materials is often lower using a separate system. The circulation of special materials is often too low to justify anything but the simplest and least costly system.

Loan Periods

Time limits are set on the length of time a borrower can keep library materials. These limits are established so that the materials will be returned within a reasonable time and made available to other users. The length of the loan period depends on the size of the collection, amount of circulation, purpose of lending materials, and the clientele served. Loan periods for most materials are one to four weeks. Special materials (such as periodicals, pamphlets, phonograph records, or films) are usually lent for shorter periods of one to seven days. These periods, of course, vary depending on the library. Libraries with smaller collections and high circulation tend to have shorter loan periods in order to make material available to as many borrowers as possible. Libraries with larger collections may allow longer loan periods. The librarian will take all of the aforementioned factors into consideration when establishing loan periods.

Some libraries limit the total number of items a patron may borrow at one time or the number of items that may be borrowed in any one subject area. This is common in smaller libraries where one patron could deplete an entire subject area unless limits were set. The larger the collection, the less need there may be to limit the borrowing.

Theft Detection Systems

Theft detection systems are in general use in academic and public libraries. The purpose of the system is to reduce theft and other types of unauthorized removal of library materials such as the patron who innocently forgets to check out material. Theft detection systems are available from several commercial vendors.

The systems operated by placing a sensitized strip or "target" in each item of library material. When materials are charged out the "target" is "desensitized" with a special piece of equipment and the patron exits normally. When a patron does not properly charge out material the sensitized "target" is detected by a sensing unit and an alarm is sounded (or a flashing light) and the turnstile gate is automatically locked. The sensing unit can detect sensitized targets even if the material is concealed.

Libraries with a theft detection system will have a policy outlining the procedures to follow when someone is caught. Because the person caught is in a "sensitive" situation, and because of possible legal consequences, library policy must be strictly followed.

The LMTA should be aware that several problems may result from the installation of a theft detection system. First, circulation staff must be aware of any materials that cannot be placed in a "desensitizing" or "sensitizing" unit. Some detection systems, for example, will scramble audio recordings (phonograph records, sound films, tapes, cassettes, etc.) when placed in the desensitizing or sensitizing unit. The LMTA must be thoroughly familiar with the system used by the library. And, second, some libraries report that mutilation of materials increases after the theft detection unit is installed. Mutilation is usually impossible to prevent, but some steps can be taken if the staff is alert to the possibility.

Patron Registration

Most libraries require patrons to register and to obtain a special identification card to charge materials out of the library. Applying for this library card is often the patron's first contact with a library. This is usually true in a public library. In academic and special libraries, however, a general identification card used for many purposes may also serve for a library card.

When a library does require the patron to register, the procedure should be simple and trouble-free. Library personnel at the registration desk must be familiar with registration procedures and prepared to answer questions about the library's services and resources. The importance of first impressions at the registration desk cannot be overstated.

Library personnel who cannot answer simple directional or informational questions or who seem annoyed with patrons' requests create a negative impression of the library that is hard to overcome. There are several important reasons for requiring patrons to register: (1) to identify persons who have the right to withdraw materials, or in some cases the right to use a library; (2) to give a patron some special form of identification necessary to charge out material or use a library—a borrower's card; (3) to obtain statistical data on the ages, occupations, interests, and geographic location of the library's users to help plan for service and acquisition of materials; this last reason applies especially to public libraries. It is important for a library to know whom it is serving and, equally important, whom it is not serving. Registration of patrons can produce useful information.

Patron registration can be handled by library clerks with overall supervision by a LMTA. The levels of personnel used for registration in a particular library will vary depending on the library's size and the attitudes of the librarians. The remainder of this chapter is an overview of registration procedures. Because daily work details vary greatly among libraries, they are not discussed here but are left to when they are best learned—while working in a library.

Public Libraries

Registration work is probably more important in a public library than in an academic or special library. As the patron's first contact with a library, the registration procedure offers an opportunity for creating good public relations. The LMTA should be aware of this opportunity and should make certain that other library personnel under his or her supervision also realize this.

An irritable, unknowledgeable, or uninterested staff member can give the patron a negative impression of the entire library. In recent years many libraries have formed library systems or entered into cooperative agreements to enable a person to charge out materials from all libraries in a geographic area by registering at any cooperating library. In at least one state a person registered in a public library can take material from any public library in the state by presenting his library card. Similarly, in some library cooperative systems registration in any library in the system gives the patron privileges in all libraries in the system. Libraries using automated circulation systems may be able to register patrons by entering information directly into the computer memory. The patron's name, address, and other information is entered using a keyboard terminal.

The patron is issued a borrower's card with a unique bar code (also called zebra code) or OCR (optical character recognition) label used to identify the patron. This is an example of a registration system being required to conform to the needs of a circulation system. Some libraries have eliminated registration and library cards. Instead, the patron uses standard forms of identification such as a driver's license, credit card, or social security card.

In small libraries, the library staff can even rely on recognizing patrons. Eliminating registration and library cards, when possible, can free much clerical staff time for other activities. Another group of patrons to be provided for are non-residents. This includes student in local colleges and universities or people temporarily working in the area, such as military personnel. Nearly every public library makes provisions for these patrons.

The same registration procedures can be used, the difference being that the library card may be dated to expire sooner than the resident's card; the card may be a different color or have other special characteristics for immediate identification. Sometimes non-residents pay a special fee, which may be refundable.

A public library may keep its own file of registered patrons or there may be a centralized file for an entire library system or geographic area. In either case an important clerical duty is to keep these files current, eliminating inactive names. Most library cards expire at regular intervals, so that people are required to register again. Files are updated when those people who do not register again are removed from the file. Some libraries have eliminated file updating by using lists of registered voters in lieu of registration, and the latest list of voters is also the list of registered library patrons.

Academic Libraries

It is remarkable that primary responsibility of the academic library is to provide service to the institution's students, faculty, and staff. Faculty and staff receive identification cards when hired and have library privileges because they work for the institution. Students are granted library privileges when they register for classes.

Students usually need one of two forms of identification in order to charge materials out of the library: (1) an identification card issued when the student registers for the academic term, or (2) a receipt for fees paid for the academic term. As a backup system, the library may have a list of currently registered students. The list is also helpful if a student does not have an identification card or receipt.

In fact, academic libraries have other special categories of users who must be registered through the library. These special users may include local school teachers and school administrators, alumni, businessmen, military personnel, and students at other institutions. The handling of each of these groups depends on local circumstances. For example, local school teachers may be allowed to charge out materials, while students from other institutions may be allowed to use materials in the library but not allowed to charge out materials. When the librarians develop a policy for non-institutional users, they always keep in mind the institution's responsibility, which is to serve its own students, faculty, and staff. The services offered to special users, therefore, are based on two factors: (1) the resources of the institution and its ability to support use by many groups, and (2) the number of special borrowers expected to use the library's resources.

Most academic libraries allow special users to use materials in the library; many do not allow them to charge out materials. There are many variations of this policy. For example, some users, such as local school teachers, are often given full library privileges, which includes charging out materials. Some academic libraries charge a fee to obtain a special borrower's card. The fee is sometimes refundable when the borrower turns in his card. The LMTA should be aware that policies for special users are not arbitrary but are based on many factors. Because the LMTA will have to answer questions about special borrower's privileges, he must be familiar with the library's policy and the reason for the policy.

Cooperation among academic libraries is helping to make their collections more easily available. One procedure is that whereby all students and faculty in an educational system are given an identification card that allows them to use any library in the system. The California State University allows students registered on any campus to have library privileges on all 19 campuses upon presentation of a valid campus identification card.

A further development is the use of cooperative agreements among academic libraries in a geographic area that allow a student registered at any institution to use the library in any other cooperating institution. Some of these cooperative arrangements include public libraries as well as academic libraries. To borrow from any library the student presents his current identification card. Sometimes a special cooperative system identification card is issued to students.

Special Libraries

Registration of patrons for special libraries can take a variety of forms. Employment with a company or government agency will give a person library privileges. Registration as a general library user in a public or academic library may also include privileges to use a special library that is part of the institution. Also, a borrower's card may be issued for a limited time to persons needing to use a special library. The temporary cards are often issued only to scholars and specialist in a particular field. There are thousands of special libraries and, of course, numerous variations in the manner of patron registration.

6

Women Library Users

Women's information needs and Library use are not the specific and predictable sort that are associated with groups whose information needs have been studied. As a group, women's needs and interests are broad and varied. In many library use situations, most usually in academic and corporate libraries, there is little useful purpose in looking at women as a category of library user. But women are the majority of public library users.

Subjects which are traditionally associated with women: cooking, needlework, home-making activities of all sorts, returning to school or work after a break as a mother/ homemaker, female health issues, and child care are the kind of practical lifestyle information that makes up much of public library reference.

There are two critical issues which women library users as a group and use of women's subjects in libraries have in common. While the users and topics make up the majority of information requests in public libraries, they are seldom covered in the professional literature of librarianship. They are not considered to be important enough or scholarly enough to be the subject of user needs research.

The problem is aggravated because public librarians are not routinely expected to do research and publish as are many academic librarians. The second critical issue is that women's information needs and the resources to meet those needs are little covered in the education of librarians. The lack of published literature on these users and their information needs makes their inclusion in the education and training curriculum difficult. There is not a body of theory that can be presented nor written materials to support teaching.

There are also significant current issues which make women library users and library users of women's subjects in timely topic for the attention of professional information workers.

Discussions of the demise of the public library in light of the "Information Highway" and potential electronic information access in all homes appear in the popular press as well as in library journals. Yet little attention is given to exactly what information the average citizen needs nor how best to deliver that information and make it useful. The issue of fee or free access to information, already difficult to resolve, is complicated by the new technology.

Transaction and use fees versus public subsidies; access for the culturally, physically, and economically disadvantaged; and copyright and legal ownership issues are all currently much discussed, but is no resolution immediately in observed.

Public Library and Practical Information

Through the first half of the twentieth century, public libraries were thought of primarily as educational and cultural institutions. Many public libraries in this country were established to help educate and prepare new immigrants for employment. Reference service was geared to assisting people with intellectual and cultural pursuits.

After World War II, public libraries began to take on an informational function. Recognition of the public library as a place where the average citizen could find information useful to his everyday needs began to appear in the professional literature with the "Information & Referral" movement in the nineteen sixties. This movement in librarianship can be traced to the Citizens Advice Bureaux often developed or housed in public libraries in Great Britain during and after World War II.

Subsequently there has been some literature on the public library as a place where people go for other practical information they need to use in their daily lives such as consumer product and service information of various kinds, recipes, nutrition information and house cleaning techniques and products, do-it-your self auto and appliance repair, parenting and child behaviour information, medical, drug, and legal information for the layperson, various kinds of information for the woman who wishes to resume education or employment after a period of full-time child rearing, etc.

Here we will make an attempt to survey the relevant publications on information needs of women and use of women's subjects and sample responses to the perceived needs. Because the potential number of topics which could be discussed in this paper is so large, the following criteria were established to limit the material to a manageable amount:

(a) neglect of the topics in the professional literature and in research,

(b) the need for discussions of the issues for educational and training materials.

(c) frequency of requests at public library. a reference desks.

Practically in the studies of general public library use in this century, women have always used libraries more than men. When use studies of particular subjects are done, women nearly always are more likely to use libraries for information on whatever subject than men.

Merchant (1991) analyzed "motivation" for adult public library use. His motivation categories were home and family life, vocational growth, religion, and politics. Among the many demographic characteristics which he included in his study was sex so that he was able to compare male and female motivation factors. Findings from this study will be mentioned as they are relevant to the various topics. Words written in the popular library press in 1982 by Parikh and Broidy are just as true today: "The population of the U.S. is over 50% female, the library profession over 80%, yet analysis of and attention to women's issues and needs both as library users and library workers lags far behind our majority representation," and "Library doors have traditionally been open to help immigrants, cultural minorities, and the economically disadvantaged gain a toehold in American society. Women in this society are an economically disadvantaged cultural minority. Today, as in the past, it is the responsibility of the public library to open its doors and extend its resources to these immigrants in a man's world."

Women's Information Needs and Use

Bates' "Library and Information Services for Women, Homemakers, and Parents" (1974) is one of the remarkable study on this theme. At that time, she wrote, "The library literature appears to be devoid of information on the needs of these three groups as groups."

Bates looked at information needs found in Extension Service surveys, women's movement organizations, and general studies of the public's information needs. Bates categorized the information needs of these groups as survival related-crisis, survival related-general, and self enrichment and growth. The first category is the library role as an "information & referral" centre for social services and various experts such as physicians, psychologists, lawyers. The second and third categories are subjects for which information can be acquired from usual public library materials. The next significant addition to the analysis of practical information needs is Dervin's 1976 chapter: "The Everyday Information Needs of the Average Citizen: a Taxonomy for Analysis." While not limited to women, her taxonomy covers many of the same subjects which Bates associated particularly with women's information needs. Dervin's complete list of subjects is neighbourhood; consumer; housing; housekeeping and household maintenance; employment; education and schooling; health; transportation; recreation and culture; financial matters or assistance; public assistance and social security; discrimination and race relations; child care and family relationships; family planning and birth control; legal; crime and safety; immigration, migration, and mobility; veterans and military; and public affairs, political, and miscellaneous. Dervin concludes by saying "The clearest generalization which emerges from this discussion is that huge gaps exist in the knowledge base relating to average citizens and their information needs."

Further few studies of specific groups of women or of

specific women's information needs have been published. One of the earlier ones is Turock's (1975) description of the establishment of a Women's Information & Referral Service in the Montclair, N.J., Public library in the 1970's. Initially, "agencies and organizations working with women were consulted to see what their primary areas of concern and assistance were."

This let to an initial data-bank on legal rights and aid, career and other counselling, family planning, self awareness, educational opportunities, day care and nursery facilities, women's organizations, and sexism in the media. However, once the service was in operation, "Most of our queries have to do with job information . . . the large majority of our patrons want to know how they can get into or return to the job market, where they can get help for writing a resume or upgrading job skills, where they can get day care for their young children." Chatman has done two studies of information needs of specific groups which are relevant to the information needs of women: one on the "working poor" (1985) and one on "older women" (1991).

Both of her studies found interesting perceptions about libraries. The women urban poor in CETA training in the earlier article did not see the library as a source of useful information specific to employment, and the older women seemed to see the library as a place to get recreational reading, but not as an information source. One of the older women had a clear picture of what she thought the library should provide:

A library can help older people by providing them with good books and things to assist them to learn. They could put out pamphlets about general tips on aging. Plus, put books on crafts in large print. They should have a newsletter for older people telling them about meetings of interest to them. If they request something special, the library should be willing to get it. I wanted a book to read so I call my daughter to pick it up for me at the library. It would be nice though if they would send it in the mail. If they weren't willing to pay for it, I would have. There are a lot of people here who have had heart attacks or are crippled. They can't get to a library. People assume that everybody can drive, and they can't. Plus older people are afraid to a lot of traffic.

Whitt (1993) studied the information needs of lesbians. The subjects of this study went to the library "for lesbian fiction, for poetry, both popular and research-oriented psychological and sociological materials and for information on ethics and sexual behaviour."

Traditional Women's Subjects

There are few use studies of stereotypical women's subjects. When such subjects are written about in library literature, the articles are nearly always on collection development, not on use or users. Traditional women's subjects, such as cooking, needlework, sewing, and gardening are rarely treated in library literature except for papers on cataloging of fiber art or preservation of textiles or in books reviews or articles on collection development. *Library Journal* has done a series on collection development of popular public library subjects including crocheting and knitting and garden design.

Chatman picked up an information need in her study of older women when one of the subjects mentioned the need for craft books in large type (see above). In addition to the technical information needs evident in the literature of these fields, there is much evidence of the need for sources of creative inspiration. For example, a much discussed topic in many of the current publications on needlework is the use of pictorial sources for design. Monitoring relevant subject lists on the Internet provides additional examples of information needs: source for unusual materials, lists of continuing education, workshops, and conferences, information on institutions, organizations, museums, etc. For the information professional this remains an unexplored area of information need and one which would prove fruit full to study.

This category is the broadest and most basic one for this paper. It includes homemakers of either sex; do-it yourself repair persons including repair of appliances, automobiles, utilities (home improvements, generally); people seeking consumer product ratings, etc.

In Merchant's (1991) categorization of adult use of public libraries, men and women were equally involved with his category, "home and family affairs," but "women were twice as likely as men to use the library for this purpose." In a study of library use for practical information, Harris and Mitchell (1988) related attitudes about bibliographic instruction to male and female sex-types topics.

They found that "The standard that seems to be operating in this study is that when patrons know little about a topic (as is apparently assumed when a patron makes a cross-sex query), the librarian is obliged to teach; yet when a patron makes a sex-consistent request, library instruction should not be given."

Female topics were day care, planning a wedding, choosing a diet, selecting a knitting pattern, and flower arranging; male topics fixing a washing machine, obtaining a patent, trout fishing,, joining the armed forces, and getting a home electrical permit. Searches through the professional literature of librarianship for practical topics frequently yield no more than one article per topic. While auto repair is a sterotypically male topic, not only are more women now repairing their own cars, but anecdotal literature tells us that women have been sent to the public library to get information on auto repair to be used by the male members of their family. The one article on auto repair, Pankl (1992), considers some aspects of information need as well as collection development. Sources of needs information outside of library literature are included. "Provision of repair manuals in public libraries is not a subject to which the professional literature of librarianship has given significant attention. An online literature search revealed no postings.

A manual search of *Library Literature* back to 1980 was almost equally fruitless. An Infotrac search revealed, however, that articles do appear in popular periodicals from time to time." Those articles in the popular do-it-yourself literature do provide information on users (e.g., surveys of which models are most worked on by owners), and state motor vehicle licensing departments can provide the number of each model licensed in the state. In preparing his discussion of the auto repair reference service at Tulsa Public Library, Pankl also surveyed nine public libraries, finding that questions on auto repair averaged 25% of total reference transactions.

Examples of other articles related to practical information for the home have less information needs content. In a collection development oriented article, Langstaff (1991), "Meet Mr. and Mrs. Fixit," quotes marketing statistics on the increase in home improvement activities by do-it-yourselfers prefatory to a discussion of the increase in publishing in this area. The one article in library literature on appliance repair manuals deal with the acquisition of those materials.

While this is clearly not a topic confined to women nearly every study of women's information needs finds this as a major, if not the highest, priority information need. Those studies include Javelin (1976) on information needs of local community organizations (women's vocational organizations), Chatman (1985) on urban poor women, Glass (1990) on minority women, and Merchant (1991) on general adult library use. Furthermore, this appears to be an area where the library is often the most frequently used information source.

The many special sections on job or career information in public libraries have increased public awareness of the library as a job information source. However, the Chatman study had less promising results. Only 36% of the subjects "considered the library as a likely source of this specific type of information. A few respondents felt that the library may have some employment-type information such as Civil Service listings and general information about a career field but no information about how one goes about pursuing a job in a specific field." A general concern was "libraries are not up to date"

This topic is also one on which the articles in the library literature uniformly deal with collection development. However, information needs on this subject have been much written about in the feminist literature; currently both the popular literature and health-care literature are very concerned with women's health research and information needs.

Parenting also is an issue which has been covered extensively in recent years in the non-library press-both popular media and sociological/psychological journals. The publishing industry has responded to this concern and many materials are available in public libraries. This topic is also one which is included in the *Library Journal* collection development series mentioned above.

The ERIC Clearing house on Assessment and evaluation announced in March 1994 the addition of fifty full-text essays on parenting to their resources. A different parental function is the frequently described practice of parents doing their children's homework in the library. While this is a common discussion topic whenever public library reference librarians are together, there has been no apparent attempt to analyze the associated information needs, and very little has been written on the topic.

Current Trends

Much of the practical kinds of information resource discussed in this paper are available for various transaction and use fees from commercial and non-profit organizations other than libraries. Those other vendors of practical information for the average citizen market their services far more extensively than do public libraries. Many people, and particularly those less able to pay, know of the fee-based services and not of the free fax-supported services. This has been a less significant issue in the past because there were not so many or so well-known fee-based alternatives. Computerization and the various network services, CompuServe, America Online, Prodigy, etc., are now making a big difference. Many more people know of and use the fee services. Far fewer know of an use the public library services.

Low -income parents peak proudly of their children accessing encyclopedias to do their homework via compuServe or Prodigy when there are comparable encyclopedias available for free computer dial-up from their local public library. Among solution to this marketing problem touted in the library press are cooperation and collaboration with other public agencies which provide information to the general citizen like Extension services and social agencies.

Maciuszko (1990) describes two kinds of organizations which go a step further, the community online systems like the Free-Nets and community online information systems organized by public libraries. The report on the Equifax-Harris Survey, *Using the Public Library in the Computer Age* (1991) also describes library-originated community computerized information systems. Without the expense of initiating a local network, some public libraries are now providing access to online information systems via the Internet.

In the 1980's public libraries provided many adults with their first lessons in computer literacy when card catalogues were converted to OPACs; they are now continuing this educational mission with providing first access to information networks for many patrons.

Library information service has always tended to rush to provide the answer before finding out the questions. Electronic information sources have not changed this sequence. Studying and analyzing the everyday information needs of women-for recreational, educational, vocational, health and family-as well as the needs of all people, regardless of sex or age or other demographic characteristics, for practical and lifestyle information has been little done. Public library administrators and jurisdictions should require research and publication on information needs of women and users of women's subjects for librarians' promotion and provide the opportunities for this research.

Public libraries and librarians need to publicize their mission of responsibility for research and publication on information needs of the average citizen rather than their popular mission as purveyors of video movies and romantic novels. Forty hours a week of frantic reference work is no longer the best way to serve the public's information needs. Perhaps the impetus provided by commercial services and home electronic access will excite librarians about pursuing such research.

REFERENCES

Alloway, Catherine S., Edward Cool, and Sherry Feintuch. "Health Index Plus: a CD-ROM Product for Consumer Health Information" *Medical Reference Services Quarterly 11* (Spring 1992) 39-45.

Bates, Marcia J. "Library and Information Services for Women, Homemakers, and parents" *in Library and Information Service Needs of the Nation: Proceedings of a Conference on the Needs of Occupational, Ethnic, and Other Groups in the United States* ed. by C.A. Cuadra and M. J. Bates (Washington, U.S. Govt. Printing Office, 1974).

Bibel, Barbara. "Consumer Health Information a Selected List of Reference Sources for the Lay User "*Booklist* 89 (Jan. 1, 1993) 828-29.

Black, M. "Homeworkers and their Information Needs" *Librarians Information Research News 16* (Spring 1993) 14-16.

Bredeson, Peggy. "Appliance Repair Manuals Sources" *Unabashed Librarian 50* (1984) 6.

Cassell, Kay Ann and Kathleen Weibel. "Public Library Response to Women and Their Changing Roles" RQ 20 (Fall 1980) 70-75.

______."Librarians, Politics, and the ERA" *Wilson Library Bulletin* 57 (Dec. 1982) 292-94.

Chatman, Elfreda A. "Channels to a Larger Social World: Older Women Staying in Contact with the Great Society" *Library and Information Science Research* 13 (1991), 281-300.

____. "Information, Mass Media Use and the Working Poor" Library and Information Science Research 7 (1985), 97-113.

Demo, Bill. "Fixing Up Your Home Repair Collection" *Library Journal 116* (Sept. 1, 1991) 161-65.

Dervin, Brenda. "The Everyday Information Needs of the Average Citizen: A Taxonomy for Analysis" *in Information for the Community,* ed. by Manfred Kochen and Joseph., C. Donohue. Chicago, A.L.A., 1976.

Doman Dave. "Community Connections: Local Information Databases" *Colorado Libraries* 18 (March 1992) 35-6.

Ensor, Pat. "P Rodigy: Bellwether or Pariah? *Online* 15 (July 1991) 61-63.

Fairer-Wessels, Felicite A. "Basic Community Information Needs of Urban Black Women" Mousaion 5 (1987) 54-65.

Geffert, Bryn. "Community Networks in Libraries: A Case Study of the Freenet P.A.T.H." *Public Libraries 32* (Mar./Apr.1993) 91-9.

Glass, Betty J. "Information Needs of Minority Women and Serials Resources: A selected Bibliography" *The Reference Librarian* 27/28 (1990) 289-303.

Harris, Jill. "The Demand for Health and Sickness Information in a Large Public Library" *NewZealand Libraries* 47 (March 1992) 3-10.

Harris, Roma M. and Gillian Michell. "Home Insulating and Home Births: Do patrons' Sex-types Questions Influence Judgements about the Competence of Reference Librarians? RQ 28 (Winter 1988) 179-84.

"Home Repair/Renovation Best Sellers" *Library Journal 117* (Apr. 1, 1992) 109.

Jackson, Mary E. "Sew Good" *Wilson Library Bulletin* 68 (Nov. 1993) 120.

Javelin, Muriel C. "Analyzing Information Needs of Local Community

Organizations: A Case Study" *Library Trends* 24 (Jan. 1976) 527-35.

langstaff, Peggy. "Meet Mr. and Mrs. Fixit" *Publishers Weekly* 238 (Oct. 4, 1991) 15-22.

Leonard, Peter C. "Remodeling a Home Renovation Collection" *Library Journal 117* (Feb. 1, 1992) 53-6.

Lind, Judith. "Threading Your way Through the Sewing Books" *Library Journal 116* (Feb. 1, 1991) 57-60.

Loorie, Nancy S. "Whose Homework is it Anyway? Helping Parents at the Reference Desk" *New Jersey Libraries* 26 (1993) 15-17.

Maciuszko, Kathleen L. "A Quiet Revolution: Community Online Systems" *Online* 14 (Nov. 1990) 24-32.

Marchant, Maurice P. "What Motivates Adult Use of Public Libraries?" *Library and Information Science Research 13* (July-Sept. 1991) 201-235.

Marshall, Joanne. "A development and Evaluation Model for a Consumer Health Information Service" *Canadian Journal of Information Science 17* (Dec. 1992) 1-17.

Murray, Joan V. "Public Libraries" *Catholic Library World 48* (Apr. 1977) 400-01.

Pankl, Robert R. "Automobile Service Information in the Public Library" *RQ* 32 (Winter 1992) 230-37.

Parikh, Neel and Ellen Broidy. "Women's Issues: The Library Response" *Wilson Library Bulletin 57* (Dec. 1982) 295-99.

Pasterczyk, Catherine E. "Hanspinning Periodicals" *Serials Review 12* (Spring 1986) 27-33.

Pritchard, Sarah M. "Linking Research Policy, and Activism: Library Services in Women's studies" *The Reference Librarian 20* (1987) 89-103.

Quint, Barbara, "Real Research for Real People" *Wilson Library Bulletin 65* (March 191) 97-100.

Turock, Betty. "Women's Information & Referral Service Asks Community for Answers" *Wilson Library Bulletin 49* (Apr. 1975) 568-72.

Van de Street, David. "Tuning Up Your Auto Repair Collection" *Library Journal 116* (June 1, 1991) 91-2.

Westin, Alan, and Anne Finger. *Using the Public Library in the Computer Age: Present Patterns, Future Possibilities.* Chicago, A.L.A., 1991.

Whitt, E. J. "The Information Needs of Lesbians" *Library and Information Science Research 15* (*Summer* 1993) 275-88.

Zlendich, Janice. "Knit One, Read, Too "*Library Journal 117* (Oct. 1, 1992) 55-9.

7

Guidelines for Locating Material

In case if your own library does not own the specific source you need, or if you just want to know what is available elsewhere on your subject, you will want to look into the holdings of other libraries. There are three steps involved:

1. Determining which specific sources exist on your subject.
2. Determining where copies of these can be found.
3. Determining which libraries have special collections on your subject, for further research or browsing.

1. The best place to start is usually your own local public or university library. The footnotes and bibliographies in the books you've located through the card catalogue and the classification scheme and the sources you've identified through the journal indexes, subject bibliographies, or databases may be enough to idenitify most of the best literature on your subject. Beyond these, however, there are several other good sources for identifying books in your area of interest; the most notable include *Book Review Digest* (with its subject index), *Subject Guide to Books in Print,* the *Cumulative Book Index,* the *BPR Annual Cumulative* and the *Library of Congress*

Catalogues: Subject Catalogue (which is now continued as a part of the microfiche *National Union Catalogue).* Each of these uses the *LC Subject Headings* list for its basic vocabulary control of subject terms.

***Book Review* Digest.** Given the avalanche of books that are available, most people will want to focus or limit their searches to a few works, at least initially. Two ways to do this are to limit either by quality of material or by recency of publication. And there are two good shortcuts to finding the quality books on a subject. One is to check several relevant encyclopaedia articles to see if their selective bibliographies mention the same works. (It is particularly useful to compare a bibliography from a specialized encyclopaedia with the one from the *Britannica,* the latter provides critical annotations to the entries in its bibliographies, which the other encyclopaedias do not).

The purpose of an encyclopaedia article is to give you a basic orientation to its subject and so its bibliography will usually try to list only the most important works. And writers of encyclopaedia articles are usually experts in their fields, so by comparing the views of two or more experts on what the important books are, you can often short-circuit some otherwise lengthy research.

The second shortcut is to use *Book Review Digest* (H. W. Wilson, 1905—). This monthly publication has annual cumulations that form a permanent set; it covers reviews appearing in 70 American, British and Canadian journals to about 6000 books every year. The important things about *BRD* are that it provides digests or extended quotations from several evaluative reviews of each book so that you can assess its critical reception from several viewpoints; and that it has a subject index.

If you start with this index, you can quickly find citations to relevant books *and* an assessment of their quality. And this works with both recent and older sources. It is sometimes advisable to use this source in addition to the encyclopaedia bibliographies, especially if these are somewhat dated.

Subject Guide to Books in Print. This is an annual set listing those works published in the United States that are currently available in bookstores or by mail. It quotes prices; and a companion set, *Title Guide to Books In Print* (there's also an *Author Guide)* gives publishers' addresses. *Subject Guide* provides an efficient way to identify the most recent books on a subject.

Its LC headings are rather broad (*i.e.*, it makes little use of the standard subdivisions to limit topics), so you will have to do some browsing for specific works. And there are companion volumes you will also want to check: *Books in Print Supplement, Subject Guide to Forthcoming Books* and *Paperbound Books in Print* (which has its own subject index). All libraries will own all of these volumes and will usually have them right next to each other in the reference department.

Cumulative Book Index (or ***CBI;*** H. W. Wilson, 1928—). This is a monthly publication with annual cumulations. Unlike *Books in Print,* which is limited to works published in the United States, the *CBI* is an ongoing record of all English language books published anywhere in the world. It lists each under author, title and subject entries, all interfiled in one alphabetical sequence.

BPR Annual Cumulative. *BPR* is the yearly hardbound cumulation of the monthly publication *American Book Publishing Record.* It is a list of books published in the United States, but it has three advantages over *Subject Guide to Books in Print.* (1) it lists entries in subject groupings according to the Dewey Decimal Classification, which greatly facilitates browsing; (2) its subject index uses *LCSH* terms *with* the subdivisions usually omitted in *Subject Guide a*nd these are very useful for fine-tuning a search or combining two or more subjects; and (3) its entries give the tracings for each book, which are very useful for suggesting related subject headings. There are large cumulations for 1876—1949, 1950—1977 and 1980—1984, with annuals thereafter.

Library of Congress Catalogues: Subject Catalogue. This is a closed set of annual and five-year cumulations; it lists alphabetically by subject heading the extensive holdings of the Library of Congress cataloged between 1945 and 1982. (As of 1983 it is superseded by the subject index to the microfiche *National Union Catalogue;* see below). It has advantages over *Subject Guide* and the *CBI* in that it reproduces the whole catalogue card for each book, enabling you to read the tracings and it is not limited to United States or English language works. Note that this is a list of what this one library actually owns—unlike the others, it is not a list of everything that has been published.

When you are doing research with any of these sources, remember that they do not provide access to three additional types of sources that are especially valuable: special collections, microform collections and government documents. (For locating special collections, see below in this chapter. Nor do they cover journal articles, which can be identified through the various indexes, bibliographies and databases.

2. The two basic sources for locating copies of books

are the *National Union Catalogue* and the OCLC computer system. They are also useful for locating journals, but for these several special union lists of serials exist that are usually better starting points. (A union list is one that records the holdings of more than one library).

The *National Union Catalogue* has two parts, composed under separate (although similar) editorial direction: there is a huge retrospective set and also a current, ongoing set that keeps the record up to date. It is worthwhile to consider the retrospective *National Union Catalogue: Pre-1956 Imprints* in some detail.

Essentially, this *Pre-'56* set is the closest thing there is to being a list of everything published worldwide from the invention of printing through the end of 1955. That's something of an oversimplification, since no such list could ever be exhaustive. But, still, the *NUC Pre-'56* is the largest list of books ever compiled: it is a 754-volume set listing about seven to nine million items that were reported to the project by over a thousand research libraries throughout North America. It is especially valuable to researchers because, for each work listed, *it tells you which libraries actually own a copy.*

Through this catalogue scholars have astonishing access to the published records of the human race, in effect "direct access to the largest, richest and most open library network in the world". Among its many other uses, the *NUC* is the foundation of interlibrary loan activity. It has been called "the best record we shall ever have of the first 500 years of man's [printed] history" and "the bibliographic wonder of the world"; and indeed it is just that. Since the set is so fundamentally important to scholarship, it is worthwhile to note in detail some of its capabilities, uses and peccadilloes—especially since these points are almost never taught in colleges and universities.

(a) The *National Union Catalogue* is basically arranged by author (not by subject), although anonymous works are included under titles. It is thus very useful for compiling a bibliography of an author's works and their various editions. (Note, however, that it does not list individual articles within journals).

(b) It lists not only books but also pamphlets, maps, atlases, broadsides, music (scores and print material rather than sound recordings), government documents, microforms and even some manuscripts. Audiovisual materials such as phonorecords, motion pictures and filmstrips are excluded, as are Braille and Moon books for the blind. Publications from all over the world are covered, although the emphasis is on works in the roman alphabet or Greek or Gaelic.

But there are also many entries in Arabic, Cyrillic, Chinese, Japanese, Hebrew, Korean, the various Indic alphabets and other non-Latin characters. The works in the Near Eastern and Oriental aiphabets are mainly those held in the vast collections of the Library of Congress.

(c) While the basic sources for determining library locations of journals and serials are the *Union List of Serials* and its supplement *New Serial Titles,* the *NUC* records some serials not listed in these; and it also covers conference proceedings and annual publications, which *ULS* and *NST* omit.

(d) The library locations for each work are designated

by symbols after the bibliographic description. The most frequently used symbols are spelled out on the inside covers of each volume. Complete lists of all the symbols can be found in three volumes, 200, 560 and 754, which are bound in brown cloth so that they will stand out from the green of the others. (A common misconception regarding the *NUC* is that the Library of Congress owns every book listed in it. This is not true; LC owns only those items that have the symbol "DLC" '—the D stands for District of Columbia).

(e) Its overall coverage is so good that book dealers frequently raise the price of any item they come across that is not listed. "Not in *NUC*" is a strong selling point for a rare book.

(f) The set provides very strong coverage of local, state and federal government documents and surprisingly good coverage of international and foreign government publications as well.

Some entries do not list locations; these are in the form of "overprinted" cards. In Figure 8, for example, a work providing David Millar Craig's biographical sketches of concert celebrities is listed under Millar Craig's name, but no library locations are listed. In this entry, however, "Millar Craig" is a typed-in (overprinted) line above the main entry "Wiener, Hilda".

When the main entry card is consulted directly, library locations are found. The overprinted entries thus serve as cross-references to main entries.

(a) If the book you want is not in the *NUC,* you should not assume that none of the participating libraries own it. Most of the institutions did not report every item cataloged in their collections, but rather concentrated on those works they considered rare or unusual. Many of the participants, in fact, contributed very few reports. Several major libraries, however—the Library of Congress, Harvard, Yale, the University of Chicago, the John Crerar and the New York Public—were extremely conscientious, reporting virtually every item cataloged in their collections. Indeed, the *NUC* lists *more* of LC's pre-1956 holdings than does LC's own public card catalogue. This is because the Library has many separate divisions that have their own catalogues and these divisional files have large numbers of items that are not recorded in the main catalogue. The *NUC* picks up some of these divisional items.

(b) The *Pre- '56 NUC* consists of *two separate* A—Z alphabets: volumes 1—685 (the main sequence) and volume 686—754 (a supplement). The main sequence contains 11,637,350 entries and cross-references; the supplement, 949,385 (for a total of 12,586,735). It is important to note that the supplement includes many corrections and additional cross-references *to the main sequence.*

(c) Each of the supplementary volumes (686—754) has a separate numerically coded section that *lists additional library locations* for works already reported in the main sequence. But you should use *both* this numeric section *and* the alphabetical section of each supplement volume when looking for additional locations of items initially reported in volumes 1—685.

(d) Each entry is usually a reproduction of a full catalogue card, including tracings. The subject headings in these can be useful in any library.

(e) The cards frequently list not only Library of Congress call numbers but sometimes Dewey Decimal numbers as well. These can help you locate browsing areas in the bookstacks of your own library. (Note, however, that call numbers given in the *NUC* may not work to retrieve the specific books you want. Even if your library uses the LC classification scheme, the tail ends of its call numbers are likely to be different from LC's numbers for the same books. In fact, it is quite possible that your own library will assign entirely different class numbers. LC class numbers, in other words, are not necessarily uniform from one library to the next).

(f) In addition to its use in locating actual copies of books and in providing tracings and classification numbers, the *NUC* is especially helpful for verifying and filling out incomplete or questionable bibliographic citations. An important point to note: if you fail to find a book under the author's name as you have it in your original citation, *try slightly variant spellings.* It is the experience of librarians who must verify hundreds of interlibrary loan requests that frequently the initial citation that readers rely on— whether it comes from a footnote, bibliography, or catalogue—is itself inaccurate. In my own work, for example, I've found in the *NUC* works by "Lessem" that were initially asked for under the name "Lessen"; "Hennig" when "Henning" was cited; and "Abern*e*thy" when the original footnote read "Abern*a*thy". This approach works *with surprising frequency.*

(g) If an author has written a book under a pseudonym, you can often use the *NUC* to find his or her real name. If you look under the pen name you will find a cross-reference to the real name.

(h) Similarly, if an author signs initials rather than his full name, you can use the *NUC* to find the full form. "Eliot, T.S". for example'. refers you to "Eliot, Thomas Sterns, 1888— ". And various entries under the latter form fill in his death date at "—1965". Similarly, you can find that Gilbert Keith Chesterton lived from 1874—1936. Such entries and dates are useful in distinguishing among authors with similar names or initials. The first and last entry under an author's name will usually provide the fullest information.

(i) The *NUC* usually provides the fastest way to find out if a foreign-language book has been translated into English. If you look under the original author's name, you will find that the entries include both original-language editions and translations. (Similarly, you can often find out whether an English language book has been translated into another language).

(j) Although as a rule works are entered under authors' names or under titles for anonymous works, there are many cross-references in the set that often allow you to find them under other points of access (*e.g.*, joint author, compiler, translator of poetry or drama, honoree of *Festschriften,* name of artist in cases of works with art reproductions). *Editors'* names, however, are usually *not* used as access points. The main entry point for most U.S. government documents (vols. 609—624) begins with the corporate designation "United States", subdivided by department, bureau, or office—but since this makes items difficult to find, the editors also included rather liberal cross-references under titles or authors' personal names for these works. Similarly, the works in the "Bible" volumes (53—56) appear rather liberally under other entry points as well. (It is noteworthy that the U.S. documents volumes and the Bible listings are such large catalogues in their own right that each has been republished as a separate set. The Bible reprin includes an index volume that cumulates the cross-references elsewhere in the *NUC*. There are also one-volume reprints of the extensive "Catholic Church" and "Freemasons" listings). Cross-references are also provided in those cases in which there is confusion or disagreement regarding the spelling of an author's name. Again, researchers should remember always to check *both* alphabets, for the supplement may contain cross-references that did not make it into the main sequence. An example is provided by Ferdinand Andre's *Deliberations de l'administration* (Mende, 1882— 1884). In the main sequence this appears only under the main entry "Lozere, France (dept).". However, if you look in the supplement under "Andre, Ferdinand" you will find a cross-reference that refers you to the "Lozere" entry.

(k) Regrettably, many books held by Pennsylvania libraries and recorded in the Union Library Catalogue of Pennsylvania are not listed in the *NUC,* due to disagreements among those involved. If you don't find an item you want in the *NUC* and wish to double-check Pennsylvania holdings—an especially wise course of action if you need to locate a work published in that state—send a stamped' self-addressed envelope with your request to the

Union Library Catalogue, 3401 Market St., Philadelphia, Pa. 19104 (215 382-5104). (Note, however, that many Pennsylvania libraries reporting their holdings to the Pennsylvania catalogue *also* reported directly to the *NUC).*

(l) All works listed in the *Pre-'56 NUC* were published, obviously, prior to 1956. However, the cut-off date for libraries to report such books was in late 1977; and about 639,000 pre-'56 publications and additional locations reported after that date did not make it into the *Pre- '56 NUC,* nor have they been included in any of the supplements after 1956 (*i.e.*, the ongoing *NUC).* The cards for this extra file still exist in a Library of Congress warehouse; however, they have not been edited or arranged in any searchable order. As of this writing no decision has been made to publish them.

(m) Researchers should be aware of seven other national union catalogues maintained in card-file format at the Library of Congress, which the regular *NUC* overlaps but does not supersede. These are for foreign-language materials in non-roman scripts; they are:

Japanese Union Catalogue (ca. 700,000 cards)

Chinese Union Catalogue (ca. 900,000 cards)

Korean Union Catalogue (ca. 110,000 cards)

Hebraic/Yiddish Union Catalogue (Ca. 500,000 cards)

Ladino Union Catalogue (ca. 9,000 cards)

Near East Union Catalogue (Arabic, Persian and Turkish; Ca. 160,000 cards)

Slavic/Cyrillic Union Catalogue (ca. 500,000 cards).

(n) These files contain entries, with library locations, for materials in non-Roman scripts *originally cataloged by libraries other than LC.* They also contain items originally cataloged by LC and which therefore appear in the regular *NUC;* but the other non-LC entries—and there are literally millions of them—are not in the *NUC.* All these card files are kept up to date, some of them with separate "Add-on" sections that cover reports received from 1981 and afterwards, which may be cataloged under different rules. The *Near East Union List* is also available in database form; and the *Slavic/Cyrillic Catalogue* is also commercially available in micro-fiche. The Library also maintains two other separate national union catalogues, one of talking books and books in Braille for blind and physically handicapped people; this exists in database form. The other, the National Union Index to Architectural Records, consists of reports of collections of architectural records throughout the country; currently it has about 1500 cards.

(o) If you want to impress a librarian with a bit of trivia, mention that you've found a circular entry in the *Pre-'56.* When you look up Kaspar Hedio's *Chronica der Alten Christlichen Kirchen* (vol. 238, p. 43, col. 3) you'll find a note to "See under Eusebius Pamphilii, bp. of Caesarea". But when you look this up (vol. 163, p. 442, col. 3) you'll find a "see" reference directing you back to "Hedio, Kaspar". (And then mention that your further research has discovered that the mistake is corrected in the supplement, vol. 773, p. 270, col. 2).

(p) If you want to be truly obnoxious in your expertise,

mention that you strongly disagree with the note written by a disgruntled *NUC* employee and inserted on the card for James Wolveridge's *Speculum Matricis* (vol. 671); and that you have grave doubts about the bibliographic veracity of entry #NP0576549 (vol. 471), which you have determined is *not* owned by the University of Oregon.

(q) The physical size of the *Pre-'56* set is staggering. Most of its 754 volumes weigh about 7½ pounds each, for a total of almost three tons. A complete set has about 528,000 pages, taking up 125 linear feet of shelving. It has been estimated that, thrown from volume 1 toward the end of the set, the world's record shot-put would reach only to volume 453; and that, had the Wright brothers' first airplane flight started at volume 1, it would have ended five feet short of the end of the set. Also, if all the 14" high volumes of one set were balanced on top of each other, the column would be over 1½ times the height of the Washington Monument.

(r) The entire *Pre-'56 NUC* is also now available in a microfiche set.

(s) One of the interesting by-products of the compilation of the set was the discovery that some widely held assumptions about research libraries are false. Gordon R. Williams, Chairman of the National Union Catalogue subcommittee within the American Library Association, has pointed out the surprising finding.

In 1901 when Librarian of Congress Herbert Putnam started the union catalogue, the implicit assumption was that—except where libraries had pursued special interests—the main differences between collections were determined by the age and size of the individual libraries in which they were housed. It was assumed that all comparable research libraries held in common virtually the same core collection and that it was essentially the older and larger libraries that were the repositories of books not generally to be found in the younger and smaller ones. This belief is implicit in Putnam's view, expressed in his annual report for 1900, that with the completion of the filing of cards from Harvard, the Boston Public Library, the New York Public Library and a few others, the union catalogue would "constitute the closest approximation now available to a complete record of books in American libraries".

The following facts, which many librarians still find difficult to believe, did not become clear until much later. Research library collections, even those of about the same age, size and purpose, hold many fewer titles in common than everyone thought. Far more titles and editions are held by only one or very few of them. And, anything even approaching a complete record of books in American libraries requires a union catalogue of hundreds of libraries.

Scholars in America are therefore especially fortunate to have a resource such as the *NUC* at their disposal—no other nation has anything like it. (The largest catalogues of other countries, *e.g.*, those for the British Library or the Bibliotheque Nationale, are not union lists; they are catalogues of only the holdings of the one national library).

3. No matter how good the coverage of the *NUC* and OCLC and the various other union lists and databases, libraries will always have many items that are recorded only on their own premises. And so you may wish to

determine which facilities simply have good collections or special holdings in your area of interest, for browsing or further research. There are two good sources for determining the existence and location of subject collections throughout the country and a third for libraries in other countries. The overall sources are:

1. *Subject Collections,* compiled by Lee Ash (New York: Bowker, revised irregularly). This is the basic guide to well over 10,000 special collections in university, college, public and special libraries and museums in the United States and Canada. Entries are arranged alphabetically according to *Library of Congress Subject Headings* (with additional subject terms as needed); each provides the address of the library, an estimate of the number of items in the collection and, frequently, descriptive notes.
2. *Directory of Special Libraries and Information Centers,* edited by Louis Lenroot-Ernt (Detroit: Gale Research, revised irregularly). This lists and describes 16,000 facilities in the United States and Canada and has a detailed subject index. A particularly useful feature is its geographic index, which will tell you quickly which iibraries are in your area.
3. *World Guide to Special Libraries,* edited by Helda Legenfelder (Munich: K.G. Saur, 1983; distributed by Gale). This lists 32,000 libraries in 159 countries. It is divided into five major categories (general, humanities, social sciences, medical/health sciences, science and technology) and has a 212-page subject index.

As with union lists, there are also many specialized

guides to libraries in particular regions within this country and to those in other countries (*e.g.*, *Special Collections in German Libraries; Subject Collections in European Libraries);* the librarians in your area can tell you which ones exist locally; the sources can be used to identify the others. The United States is particularly blessed with an excellent interlibrary loan (ILL) network. If you cannot find the book or article you want within your area, be sure to ask your librarians about the possibilities of borrowing the item from another facility, or of acquiring a photocopy. It is best to first ask through a library; if this doesn't work, or if the item cannot be borrowed or photocopied through interlibrairy loan, then. contact the holding institution directly. Sometimes it will have photocopy or microfilming procedures outside the ILL network; or it can give you the names of local researchers for hire who can make photocopies for you. The overall point to keep in mind is that if you have identified a good source that is not available in your local library, don't give up. The same local library is likely to have the means of identifying which other libraries either have the desired item or are likely to have it.

8

Some Legal Issues

IRS Regulations

Libraries of all types receive gifts from time to time. Some gifts are useful and occasionally even very valuable; however, much of the time they are of little interest to the library. Nevertheless, the individuals giving the material generally believe that it is very valuable. People often expect, what, and/or request a document from the library indicating the value of their gift.

Valuing Gifts

One of the IRS regulations relevant to libraries has to do with gifts and donations to a library or not-for-profit information center. Any library, or its parent institution, that receives a gift-in-kind (books, journals, manuscripts, and so forth) with an appraised value of $5,000 or more must report the gift to the IRS. A second regulation forbids the receiving party (in this case the library) to provide an estimated value for a gift-in-kind. A third disinterested party or organization must make the valuation. The latter requirement grew out of concern that recipients were placing unrealistically high values on gifts. The donor received a larger tax deduction than was warranted, and it did not cost the receiving organization anything to place a high value on the gift.

Normally, an appraiser charges a fee for valuing gifts, and the donor is supposed to pay the fee. Most often, the appraisers are antiquarian dealers who charge a flat fee for the service unless the collection is large or complex. If the appraisal is complex, the appraiser charges either a percentage of the appraised value or an hourly fee. Typically, with gifts thought to be lees than $4,999 in value, the library may write a letter of acknowledgement indicating the number and type of items received. For gifts of less than $250, the IRS does not require a letter. The donor can set a value on the gift for tax purposes. (The best practice is to provide a letter for any accepted gift.) If asked, the library can provide dealer catalogs so that donors can review retail prices for items similar to their donation. However, the final value of the gift is established by the donor and her or his tax accountant. *Note:* The collection development staff should be involved in the acceptance of gifts and must have a sound knowledge of material prices. Just because the gift is small in terms of number of items does not mean that the fair market value is below $5,000.

Recently, Loyola Marymount University (LMU) received a gift of 483 books about Japanese art, architecture, and landscape design; its appraised value was $39, 743. The donor might well have accepted a letter simply stating the number of books given and thus have lost a substantial tax deduction.

To meet IRS requirements, an acknowledgment letter must contain the library's name, the date of the contribution, and the location or place of the gift. At a minimum, that description should state the number and kind of gift.

Publishers' Inventories

Another IRS regulation or ruling (the *Thor power Tool* decision) had some influence on acquisition practices in the 1980s and early 1990s. The ruling overturned a longstanding practice common in business (including the publishing industry), which was writing down the value of inventories to a low level each year. The practice produced a paper loss that the firm deducted from its income, thus reducing tax liability.

The U.S. Supreme Court, deciding that this was taking a current deduction for an estimated future loss, said the practice was inappropriate. Only if the inventory is defective or if there is objective evidence that the firm offered the inventory for sale below cost could it employ the write-down. What does the *Thor* decision have to do with collection development? Publishers who followed the write-down practice claimed it was the only way they could afford to publish small runs of books expected to sell slowly (four to five years to sell out the first printing). Publishers talked about destroying some of their stock, and some did. In 1981 and 1982, jobbers indicated that they had received increased OP and OS reports from publishers. Blackwell North America stated in a promotional flyer in mid-1981, "[We] are receiving more o.p., o.s. and generally non-reports, than ever before. In fact, our reports to libraries on unavailable titles have increased 47 percent over a year ago." There was some hope that the U.S. Congress might pass some legislation exempting publishers. What probably helped resolve the concern was the 1987 tax reform act. Though it did not address the question of inventories, the act did reduce corporate tax rates, thus reducing the need to find deductions. Concern has decreased, but publishers appear to declare items out of print more quickly now than before the *Thor* decision.

No one is certain whether there has been a decline in short-run titles published or whether such a decline, if it exists, is the result of the *Thor* decision or of a changing economy. The decision does mean that librarians should not count on finding this year's imprints available in a year or two. In the past, a library might well have decided not to buy some current items, thinking that they could be ordered in year or two, when funding would be better. Today, it is probably best to buy materials now rather than wait.

In 1990, Ambassador Book Service (a book jobber located in New York state), in response to librarian concerns about the increasing problem of OP and OS reports, issued some fact sheets. One sheet, based on data from the on-line version of *Books in Print* (*BIP*), showed books published, in print and out-of-print for an 11-year period (1979-1989). The table illustrated what everyone knows: the percentage of out-of-print materials increases the farther back in time one goes. However, 81.9 percent of the titles listed in the 1979 *BIP* were available in 1984, and 46.9 percent were available in early 1990. Acquisition or collection development common knowledge was that most books go out of print within four to five years.

Which was right, the vendor's data or librarians' common knowledge? Both are right and wrong. The vendor's data is correct, as far as it goes-that is, items listed in *BIP*. When one considers that libraries acquire a wide range of items not in *BIP*, including small and regional press titles, report literature, scholarly society publications, and so forth, the picture changes. Without doubt, there has been an increase in items going OP. In many cases, the slowing economy and library cutbacks on monographic purchases caused small publishers (private or professional) to reduce press runs.

Copyright

IS copyright an issue in collection development? yes/

Cooperative collection development efforts depend on sharing resources through interlibrary loan or other reciprocal borrowing agreements. There are also questions about how many photocopies one can use for course reserve purposes in educational institutions. What about making a copy of an out-of-print work for preservation purposes: how does the copyright law affect these programs? Clearly, libraries have modified copying policies as well as interlibrary loan practices. For example, under the present law, a library in a not-for-profit setting may borrow no more than five articles per year from any given journal. If the library borrows more than five articles, the assumption is that the borrowing is in lieu of placing a subscription and thus is a violation of the law. If libraries may not freely exchange books, periodicals, or photocopies of copyrighted items, it will be difficult to develop effective cooperative systems. Copyright grants the creators of works certain rights that protect their interest in the work. Originally, copyright's purpose was to provide protection against unauthorized printing publishing, importing, or selling of multiple copies of a work. In essence, it was protection from the unauthorized mass production and sale of a work. It was a straightforward and seemingly reasonable method of encouraging individuals or businesses to take a financial risk to produce and distribute information. Libraries, in contrast, exist to disseminate information on a mass, usually free, basis.

Until photocopiers appeared on the scene, the relationship between copyright holders and libraries was cordial, if not always friendly.

With the development of fast, inexpensive photocopying, problems arose. Though the library might make only a single copy for a customer, the aggregate number of copies could be very high. By the mid-1960s, the volume of copying was so great that copyright holders became convinced that libraries, schools, and individuals were violating their rights-and in some cases they were correct.

In the past, copying printed matter for personal use was no problem. Word-for-word hand-copying of extensive sections of books or complete magazine articles was uncommon-people took notes. Today, quick, inexpensive copy services, as well as the ability to download digitized copyrighted material, exist everywhere. All of us have made photocopies of complete journal articles or printed many pages of Internet material rather than take notes; some of those items were from current issues of periodicals that we could have purchased for not much more than the cost of the copied item. All of us have done it and, if we thought about it at all, we thought that just one copy isn't going to hurt anyone. Unfortunately, as the number of such copies and printing increases, so does the problem.

With audiovisual materials (for example, video-tapes and audiotapes), the problem is acute. Institutions and individuals who own the hardware to play these materials also have copying capabilities. Control of copying is even more difficult to achieve for audiovisual materials than for books or journals. Preview copies help control the institutional buying situation, because they tend to show wear to such an extent that many persons would not want to reproduce a copy. If the preview copy shows too much wear, however, the library's buyer may decide not to buy the item because it lacks technical quality,

The public still does have some rights to gain access to and to use copyrighted material. Where to draw the line between creators' and users' rights is a complicated problem, and has become more so with digitization of material and scanning devices. An old but still valid editorial by J.

Berry in *Library Journal* summed up the complex issues involved in fair use.

Remarkably, many points about copyright bear emphasis, First, the problem of how to handle the rights of creators and users is worldwide, in the sense that each country has to deal with both its own copyright problems and international copyright issues, Second, in the past much of the controversy centered on educational and library copying. Today, with computer technology so readily available, the problem has increased far beyond libraries and educational institutions.

Third, copyright disputes divide authors, publishers, and producers from libraries, schools, and users, almost destroying what were once friendly working relationship. The relationship has not yet deteriorated to the point of hostility, but unless true compromises emerge, hostility may be the result. Most librarians agree that creators' rights need and deserve protection and that those rights have occasionally been violated in any by libraries. However, direct daily contact with users and their needs tempers that recognition.

There is no question that some people copy materials for commercial purposes, especially music and video products. However, much of the "improper" usage is a function of not understanding the nature of copyright and what fair usage may be in various circumstances. There are many misconceptions about copyrights and we can only touch on a few of them.

One of the most common misunderstandings of copyright concerns notice of copyright. ("It did not indicate that it was copyrighted, so it must be public domain.") Part of the reason for confusion about the need to have a notice of copyright is because, in the United States, it *was* necessary until April 1, 1989. After that date, the United States joined most of the rest of the world as a signatory to the Berne copyright convention, which grants copyright with or without notice. Thus, the only safe assumption now is that everything is copyrighted, unless one has definite knowledge that it is not covered.

A related technical misconception is that if an item is on Usenet, it is public domain. For anything to be in the public domain, the creator or owner must include a statement putting the material into the public domain.

There is also a common belief that if one does not charge for a gain financially from the usage, there is no violation of copyright. We noted earlier that libraries should also purchase performance rights for the films and videos they purchase, if they are to be used in library programming. Even a free "public performance" during a children's program requires permission, if one did not pay for performance rights. Use in face-to-face instruction has been thought to be "fair use," but even that idea is questioned by many copyright holders. As we mentioned, it is better to acquire performance rights if at all possible.

Fair use is an area full of "yes, you can/no, you can't." Now that the United States has passed the Digital Millennium Copyright Act, the issue of what will and will not deemed fair use is unclear, as of mid-1999. (We explore this concept further later in this chapter.) Older guidelines seem to be under scrutiny and the goal appears to be a further lessening of fair use rights.

Another aspect of the situation seems to be peoples' attitudes. There appears to be a sense that infringing copyright is not really a crime. The attitude think that it *really is okay to drive* 70 miles per hour. Related to that belief, which is inaccurate, is the notion that copyright holders are greedy and that the cost for permission to use copyrighted material is much too high. Therefore, using the material without permission is reasonable. Legally, it is not okay either to exceed the speed limit or to infringe copyright, even if no one is looking.

Libraries are caught in the middle of these issues. Librarians may agree that prices are high, but they also know that if there was no income and profit for the producers there would be no information. They believe in free access to information, especially for educational purposes, once the library acquires the material or information. Finding the balance, or John Berry compromise, is the challenge. In many ways, the only organized voice for users if library and educational associations.

As noted earlier, producers need encouragement to risk creating something new and making it available. Without adequate incentives, the producer will not produce. For publishers and media producers, copyright is one of the most important incentives. In essence, copyright states: "Person (s) *X* owns this creation; if you are not person (s) *X*, before you make copies of this creation for more than your own personal use, you must get written permission from person(s) *X*."

England was the first country to legalize creative ownership; in 1710, the England Parliament passed the Statute of Anne, the first copyright bill. This law did two things: it gave parliamentary recognition to a royal decree of 1556, and it gave legal recognition of a work's author as the ultimate holder of copyright. Whereas contemporary copyright laws exist to encourage the creation of new, original works and to encourage their wide public distribution, the 1556 decree had a less noble purpose: repression of the freedom of religion-in this case, the Protestant Reformation. Censorship, rather than free public dissemination of information and thought, was the goal. Without question, the Statute of Anne was a notable piece of legislation that did more than merely give legal sanction to censorship. Although by 1710 authors and publishers were allies in the fight to retain or gain more control over the use of their creations, it was an uneasy alliance, because the authors were the true creators of the copyrighted works. As the creators, authors thought they should have a greater share and say in the distribution of their works, and they thought the profits should be more evenly divided. Before 1710, all rights resided with the publisher. With the enactment of the Statute of Anne, authors received a 14-year monopoly on the publication of their works. An additional 14-year monopoly was possible if the author was still living at the end of the first term. Thus, for 28 years, the creator of a work could benefit from its publication.

The British colonies in North America developed a copyright concept based on the English model. Indeed, the concept was so much a part of American legal thought that it become part of the U.S. Constitution, wherein Congress was given the power "to promote the Progress of Science and Useful Arts, by securing for limited Times to Authors and Inventors the exclusive ending in 1891, Congress passed legislation granting exclusive rights to American authors and their representatives, but it refused to grant copyright to nonresident foreign authors. In 1831, Congress passed an act extending the copyright term: the new first term was for 28 years, though the second term remained 14 years. Extension of the exclusive rights has been of concern in all countries since the start of the nineteenth century.

By 1870, copyright also covered art prints, musical compositions, photographs, "works of fine arts," translation rights, and the right to dramatize nondramatic works. In 1887, performance rights for plays and musical compositions received coverage. The Chace Act of 1891 finally granted copyright to nonresident foreign authors, if their work was published in English and was printed in the United States.

In 1909, Congress passed a new copyright act that was a matter of extended debate from 1905 to 1909. (Since 1909, each time a revision in copyright law has been put forward, the length of debate time has increased, as has the number of groups wanting to have their voices heard.) Several important issues remained unresolved in 1909, including libraries' rights to import books printed in foreign countries and the use of copyright music on mechanical instruments, such as phonograph records and piano rolls. After considerable debate, libraries and musicians received the desired rights. Libraries could import a limited number of copies of a foreign work, and copyright owners were to receive payment for the use of their music in mechanical devices. (The later development of jukeboxes, not covered by the 1909 law, caused another problem. When a new technology, the jukebox, appeared on the scene, there was no legal mechanism for requiring payment to copyright owners for the repeated use of their works in the new devices, which were making substantial profits for jukebox owners.)

Composers worried about technological developments in 1909; in the 1970s, authors and publishers worried about technological developments. Today, everyone worries about technology and copyright. Other provisions of the 1909 law (as passed and amended over the years) included coverage of motion pictures; allowance to the owner of a nondramatic literary work to control public renditions of the work for profit and to control the making of transcriptions or sound recordings of the work; granting of full copyright protection to foreign authors (this was done so the United States could join the Universal Copyright Convention in 1954) coverage of all sound recordings; extension of copyright terms to two terms of 28 years each, with a renewal requirement for the second term; and requirement of a notice of copyright to be displayed on all works.

Several of these provisions created barriers for American and foreign producers and made it difficult for the United States to be an effective member of a worldwide copyright program. The three major stumbling blocks have been term of protection, the renewal requirements, and the manufacturing clause (i.e., the requirement that works of foreign authors be printed in the United States in order to be protected).

Now a look at some international copyright conventions.

International Copyright Conventions

At the international level, there have been two important copyright conventions: the Berne Convention (1886) and the Universal Copyright Convention (1952). Until the signing of the Berne Convention in 1886, international copyright was in chaos, with reciprocity only on the basis of bilateral treaties. Some countries, like the United States, made no such agreements. As a result, during the nineteenth century, a new form of piracy appeared: literary piracy. Some countries signed the Berne Convention, with notable exceptions being the United States and Russia. Basically, the signatories agreed to give one another the same copyright protection they provided their own citizens. A 1908 revision required this coverage to be automatic-copyright owners did not have to file any forms to secure coverage. The Internet brought chaos back to copyright, as different countries have very different concepts of fair use (U.S.) or fair dealing (U.K.)

The United States did sign the Universal Copyright Convention (UCC) in 1954. How is it that the United States was able to sign. one international convention but not the other? There were two important differences between the conventions. First, the UCC did not provide automatic copyright without formalities. The formalities, however, were that a work carry the copyright symbol), the name of the owner, and the date of first publication. That satisfied the U.S. notice requirement and, presumably, made life easier for American librarians. The second difference was that the term of copyright could be whatever term the country granted its citizens at the time of signing; the only minimum was 25 years for all works other than photographs and applied arts.

In 1971, modifications to both the Berne Convention and the UCC ensured that developing countries would receive certain licensing rights. The revisions provided a mechanism for forcing a copyright owner to grant use rights to developing countries under certain conditions-in effect, it was compulsory licensing. Most of the signatories to the two conventions approved the revisions by 1990. Certainly, the revisions helped control what was becoming the second ear of international piracy of literary and creative works. Nevertheless, some countries are not party to any copyright agreement, not do the publishers in those countries bother to seek a license; hence, piracy is still alive in the 1960s.

Practically, to understand current U.S. copyright law,

it is also necessary to look at and understand the international aspects of intellectual property protection. This is because the 1998 Digital Millennium Copyright Act (DMCA) was in part motivated by the need to conform to new international requirements.

In fact, there were two major international conventions. The Berne Convention members set up an administrative group to handle its activities. That group evolved into today's World Intellectual Property Organization (WIPO), which is also one of the United Nation's specialized agencies. WIPO has 171 member countries and administers 21 treaties. Two of its goals are to "harmonize national intellectual property legislation and procedures," and to "marshal information technology as a tool for storing, accessing, and using valuable intellectual property information."4 (*Intellectual property* in this case of WIPO means industrial property , such as inventions, trademarks, and industrial design; and copyright covering such material as literary, musical, artistic, photographic, software [as a literary work] databases, and audiovisual works).

Digital Millennium Copyright Act

The purpose of the DMCA was to update existing U.S. copyright law in terms of the digital world, as well as to conform to the 1996 WIPO treaties. Congress also passed a Copyright Term Extension Act in 1998, which added 20 years to the protection term for both individuals and corporate bodies. The old protection terms were life plus 50 years for individuals and 75 years for corporate entities. (There was an exception for libraries, archives, and non-profit educational institutions during the last 20 years of protection. Essentially, these groups would have greater fair usage during the last 20 years, if the work was not commercially available. One must wonder just how often that will be necessary. How many requests do libraries receive for special fair usage of material that is 70 years old?)

The 1978 copyright law is still in force, but changed dramatically as a result of amendments and the DMCA. The fair use doctrine is given statutory recognition for the first time in the 1978 law. Traditionally, fair use has been a judicially created limitation on the exclusive right of copyright owners, developed by the courts because the 1909 copyright law made no provision for any copying. In the law, fair use allows copying of a limited amount of material without permission from, or payment to, the copyright owner (107).

The law extends copyright protection to unpublished works. Instead of the old dual system of protecting works under common law before publication and under federal law after publication, the law establishes a single system of statutory protection for all works, whether published or unpublished (301).

A five-member Copyright Royalty Tribunal exists to review royalty rates and to settle disputes among parties entitled to several specified types of statutory royalties in areas not directly affecting libraries (801).

Every librarian should have some knowledge of all of the following sections of the law. The sections of the law and the content of handbooks on the law can be helpful in developing a collection; however, when questions arise, the best source of information is an attorney who handles copyright cases.

What follows *is not* legal advice—merely an outline of the sections and their content:

- 102-105 define works protected by copyright.
- 106 define the exclusive rights of the copyright owner.
- 107 establishes the basis of the right of fair use.
- 108 authorizes certain types of library copying.
- 108 (g) identifies library copying not authorized by the current law.
- 602 (a) (3) relates to the importation of copies by libraries.

Works Protected by Copyright

Copyright protection extends to *literary* (including computer software) works; *dramatic* works; *pantomimes* and *choreographic* works; *pictorial, graphic,* and *sculptural* works; *motion pictures* and other *audiovisual* works; and *sound recordings* (102).

Unpublished works by U.S. and foreign authors receive protection under the copyright statute, as do published works by U.S. authors. The published works of foreign authors are subject to copyright under certain conditions, including coverage under national treaties such as the Universal Copyright Convention (104) and now the WIPO Copyright Treaty.

United States government works are not copyrightable. The law did not change the basic premise that works produced for the U.S. government by its officers and employees are not subject to copyright (105).

Exclusive Rights of Copyright Owners

Section 106 states the exclusive rights of copyright owners. Subject to 107 through 118, the owner of copyright under this title has the exclusive rights to do and to authorize any of the following:

1. To reproduce the copyrighted work in copies or phonorecords.
2. To prepare derivative works based upon the copyrighted work.
3. To distribute copies or phonorecords of the copyrighted work to the public by sale or other transfer of ownership, or by rental, lease, or lending.
4. In the case of literary, musical, dramatic, and choreographic works, pantomimes, and motion pictures and other audiovisual works, to perform the copyrighted work publicly.
5. In the case of literary, musical, dramatic, and choreographic works, pantomimes, and pictorial, graphic, or sculptural works, including the individual images of a motion picture or other audiovisual work, to display the copyrighted work publicly.

It is important to understand the significant limitations on the exclusive rights stated in 106, which are stated in 107 through 118.

Fair Use

In the last edition of this book we wrote, "Even the most adamant copyright holder advocate acknowledges that at least some kinds of copying are fair and permissible. The problem lies in defining what constitutes fair use."

Although the existing law did recognise fair use, copyright holders have become less and less happy with the concept. Reading statements from representatives of copyright holders over the decade makes one wonder how long "fair use" will exist. For example, in 1992, the Association of American Publishers asserted:

> The copyright law provided the copyright holder with the exclusive right to control the making of copies of a copyrighted work. Exceptions to the exclusive right are intended to permit limited, occasional copying for individuals in particular circumstances which will not impair the rights of the copyright holder, nor generate regular business-like activities based upon usurpation of copyright owners' rights, markets, or materials.

Richard Schockmel commented about the AAP statement in a 1996 article on fair use and use fees:

> [T]his 1992 AAP statement.... in effect nullifies fair use: Copyright holders have exclusive rights to control all copying and no exceptions are allowed which would impair these rights. It is difficult to imagine any copying made without permission and/or fee which would not impair the exclusive right to control making copies.

Perhaps a more worrisome statement is that of Marybeth Peters, U.S. Register of Copyrights, in a 1998 interview with *Library Journal* staff. She was asked about ALA's concern that proposed changes in the law would mean that fair use would not exist in the twenty-first century. Her response was, "I disagree. What the library community is arguing is that is a copyright owner employs technological protection measures to safeguard his work, they may never be able to get around that protection to exercise their fair use rights. My point is you can't argue fair use to get access to a work." Later in the interview she said, "Fair use is a defense to copyright infringement to the unauthorized exercise of any of the exclusive rights of a copyright owner." We are not clear how exercising the permission given in 107 for fair use is a defense against infringement, but then we are not lawyers. She went on to say, in relation to what was to become the DMCA, "That is why the act of circumventing a technological protection measure that prevents unauthorized exercise of any of the copyright owners' rights *is not* pròhibited. For example, if a librarian obtained legal access to a work.

If all of that seems confusing, it is because the matter is confusing. It is also the reason there are ongoing discussions about the concept. Attempts have been made to help define what really constitutes fair use. After passage of the 1976 law, the Conference on Technological Use (CONTU), drawing on the House Judiciary Committee report, develop some guidelines. Though helpful, neither users nor owners have been pleased with its results as technology evolved. Another effort, in 1994, by the Conference on Fair Use (CONFU), attempted to resolve some of the technological concerns. (Several groups—for example, the American Association of University Professors and Association of American Law Schools—had opposed the existing guidelines as not representing the needs of higher education well).

CONFU negotiators spent two years developing the report they issued in 1996. The proposed guidelines generated expressions of concern from a substantial number of educational organisations, unlike the earlier guidelines. Perhaps the most important point to keep in mind is that the fair use guidelines do *not* have the force of law. They are only interpretations of the law and they are not the only possible interpretation. A good article on this issue is Kenneth Crews's "Fair Use and Higher Education : Are Guidelines the Answer?"

Fair use doctrine was codified in general terms in 107. That section refers to such purposes as criticism, commentary, news reporting, teaching, scholarship, or research, and it specifies four criteria to use in determining whether a particular instance of copying or other reproduction is fair. The statutory criteria in 107 are :

1. the purpose and character of the use, including whether such use is of a commercial nature or is for non profit educational purposes.
2. the nature of the copyrighted work.
3. the amount and substantiality of the portion used in relation to the copyrighted work as a whole.
4. the effect of the use upon the potential market for or value of the copyrighted work.

Depending on the circumstances, fair use might cover making a single copy or multiple copies. For example, multiple copying for classroom use may be considered fair use under certain circumstances. In deciding whether any particular instance of copying is fair use, one must always consider the statutory fair use criteria.

Guidelines for Copying

The 1976 Guidelines developed by educators, publishers, and authors provided some indication of what various parties believe is reasonable fair use. The guidelines are not apart of the statute, but they are part of the House Judiciary Committee's report on the copyright bull. They are *Guidelines for Classroom, Copying in Not-for-Profit Educational Institutions* and *Guidelines for Educational Uses of Music.* As noted earlier, there is much debate about fair use and use of the guidelines as "safe harbours". However, until there is a clear court decision or Congress clarifies the meaning of fair use, the guidelines are all that users have to go by.

Library Copying Authorized by Section 108

In addition to copying that would fall within the fair use section of the statute, certain types of library copying that may not be considered fair use are authorized by 108. Section 108 in no way limits the library's fair use right (108(f)(4)).

Section 108(a) contains general conditions and limitations that apply to the authorized copying outlined in the rest of the section. These general conditions apply:

1. The copy is made without any purpose of direct or indirect commercial advantage.
2. The collections of the library are open to the public or available not only to researchers affiliated with the library but also to other persons doing research in a specialized field.
3. The copy includes a notice of copyright.

The House Judiciary Committee's report clarified the status of special libraries in for-profit institutions with respect to the criterion "without direct or indirect commercial advantage" (108(a)(1)). It is the library or archives within the institution that must meet the criteria, not the institution itself.

Besides the general conditions of 108(a), it is possible for contractual obligations between a publisher or distributor and a library to limit copying that would otherwise be permissible under 108. Furthermore, the limited types of copying authorized by 108 can be augmented by written

Possible Contractual Limitations on Section 108

Section 108(f)(4) states that the right of reproduction granted to libraries do not override any contractual obligations assumed by the library when it obtained a work for its collection. In view of this provision, librarians must be especially sensitive to the conditions under which they purchase materials. Before executing an agreement that would limit their rights under the copyright law, they should consult with legal counsel. *This is the key section with regard to licensing agreements.*

Single Copy of Single Article or Small Excerpt

Section 108(d) authorizes the making of a single copy of a single article or a copy of a small part of a copyrighted work in the library's collections, provided that (1) the copy becomes the property of the user; (2) the library has no notice that the use of the copy would be for any purpose other than private study, scholarship, or research; and (3) the library both includes on its order form and displays prominently at the place where users submit copying requests a warning about copyright in accordance with requirements prescribed by the register of copyrights.

Notice: warning concerning copyright restrictions

The copyright law of the United (Title 17, United States Code) governs the making of photocopies or other reproductions of copyrighted material.

Under certain conditions specified in the law, libraries and archives are authorized to furnish a photocopy or other reproduction. One of these specified conditions is that the photocopy or reproduction is not to be "used for any purpose other than private study, scholarship, or research." If a user makes a request for, or later uses, a photocopy or reproduction for purposes in excess of "fair use," that user may be liable for copyright infringement.

This institution reserves the right to refuse to accept a copying order if, in its judgment, fulfilment of the order would involve violation of copyright law.

Copying for Interlibrary Loan

Section 108(d) authorizes the making of a single copy of a single article or a copy of a small part of a copyrighted work for purposes of interlibrary loan, provided that it meets all the conditions previously listed regarding a single copy of a single article from the library's own collections, and further provided (108(g)(2)) that requests for interlibrary loan photocopies are not in such aggregate quantities as to substitute for purchases or subscriptions. The wording of the statute places responsibility for compliance on the library requesting the photocopy, not on the library fulfilling the request. The National Commission on New Technological Uses of Copyrighted Works (CONTU), in consultation with authors, publishers, and librarians, developed guidelines to assist libraries in complying with this provision, A library or archive may receive no more than five photocopy per year of articles published in the restricted issues of a periodical. (They may be five copies of one article or single copies of five different articles.) The restriction applies only to issues published within the last five years. Duplication of older issues is limited only by the broad provisions of 108(g)(2), which prohibit copying that by its nature would substitute for a subscription. We should note that not all journal publishers agree with those guidelines. Also, in 1997 there was a ruling that has clouded the picture, at least for document delivery services.

Coin-Operated Copying Machines

Section 108(f)(1) and (2) make it clear that *neither libraries nor library employees are* liable for the unsupervised use of reproducing equipment (this does include microform reader/printers) located on library premises, if the machine displays the required notice. The person making the copy is, of course, subject to liability for copyright infringement, if his or her copying exceeds the provisions of 107.

Library Copying Not Authorized by Section 108

With the exception of audiovisual news programs, 108 does not authorize a library to make multiple copies. Two general types of library copying that are not clearly defined in the statute are specifically not authorized by 108. Stated only in the most general terms, the definitions of these types of library copying are susceptible to many interpretations.

The first is "related or concerted reproduction or distribution of multiple copies." This related or concerted copying by libraries is illegal, whether the library makes the copies all on one occasion or over a period of time, and whether the copies are intended for aggregate use by one individual or for separate use by individual members of a group (108(g)(1)).

The second type of library copying not authorized by 108 is "systematic reproduction or distribution of single or multiple copies." Because many librarians feared that this term might preclude a wide range of interlibrary lending systems, Congress amended this section of the bill to clarify that whatever may be meant by the term *systematic,* copying for purposes of interlibrary loan as specifically authorized by 108(d) is not illegal under 108(g)(2) as long as it does not substitute for purchases or subscriptions. The wording of the statute places responsibility for copyright compliance on the library requesting the photocopy, not on the library filling the request (108(g)(2)).

Importation of Copies by Libraries

In general, the law prohibits the importation of copies of works without the permission of the copyright holder. There are, however, certain exceptions to this general prohibition, one of which directly, relates to libraries.

Section 602(a)(3) states that a non-profit scholarly, educational, or religious organization may import no more than one copy of an audiovisual work for archival purposes only, and no more than five copies of any other work "for its library lending or archival purposes, unless the importation of such copies or phonorecords is part of an activity consisting of systematic reproduction or distribution, engaged in by such organization in violation of the provisions of Section 108(g)(2)."

Infringement

A person who violates the rights of the copyright owner is a *copyright infringer*. Remedies available to the copyright holder for infringement include damages (actual or statutory; the latter set by statute at from $100 to $100,000 per infringement), injunction, and recovery of court costs and attorney's fees. There is also criminal infringement (done wilfully for commercial advantage or private financial gain), which is subject to a $10,000 fine and/or one year imprisonment per infringement.

There is a waiver of statutory damages for a library or non-profit educational institution when the institution, or one of its employees acting within the scope of his or her employment, "believed or had reasonable grounds for believing that his or her use of the copyrighted work was a fair use under Sec. 107 (504(c)(2)).

Librarians and media specialists have a professional responsibility to learn about provisions of the copyright law that relate to libraries and to frequently review their practices in light of such provisions. If current practices seem likely to constitute infringement, librarians should plan now for needed changes and make sure that library users understand the reason for such changes. Above all, it is important to take the tie and trouble to master the basic provisions of the statute, so the library will fully exercise the rights it has under the copyright law. Anything short of this would be a disservice to library users.

DMCA and Technology Issues

Earlier we noted that the DMCA amended U.S. law to comply with WIPO treaties. It did more than that; it also addressed a great many of the technology aspects of copyright.

One of the education/library community's concerns about the decline of fair use rights related to 1201. This section prohibits gaining unauthorized access to material by circumventing any technological protection measures a copyright holder may have put in place. The implementation of this section is to begin two years after the legislation became law-about the end of 2000. During this two-year period, the Library of Congress is to conduct a rule making procedure to determine what, if any, exceptions would be appropriate. LC then must conduct similar proceedings every three years.

Section 1201 is not intended to limit fair use, but fair use is *not* a defense to circumventing technological protection measures. These other elements in the section have limited implication for collection development, at least at the time we wrote this chapter.

Section 1202 prohibits tempering with "Copyright Management Information" (CMI). The DMCA identified the following as constituting copyright management information:

- Information that identifies the copyrighted work, including title of the work, the author, and the copyright owner.

- Information that identifies a performer whose performance is fixed in work, with certain exceptions.
- Terms and conditions for use of the work.
- Identifying numbers or symbols that accompany the above information of links to such information; for example, embedded pointers and hypertext links.
- Such other information as the Register of Copyrights may prescribe by regulation, with an exception to protect the privacy of users.

One aspect of the DMCA that will probably be very important to libraries is "Title II: Online Service Provider Liability." The reason for this is that the DMCA defines "online service provider" (OSP) very broadly, and libraries that offer electronic resources or Internet access could be considered OSPs. The lawa creates some "safe harbors" for certain specified OSP activities. When an activity is within the safe harbor, the OSP qualifies for an exemption from liability. One should read the most current material available about this title, as it is complex and legal interpretation of it is likely to evolve.

Title IV provides some clarification about library and archival digitization activity for preservation purposes. It allows the creation of up to three digital preservation copies of an eligible copyrighted work and the electronic loan of those to qualifying institutions. An additional feature is that it permits preservation, including in a digital form, of an item in a format that has become obsolete.

Distance education activities are also addressed in Title IV. The Register of Copyright is to provide Congress with a report on "how to promote distance education through digital technologies." Part of the report is to address the value of having licenses available for use of copyrighted works in distance education programs. (The DMCA was only six months old at the time we prepared this chapter.)

After their success against for-profit organizations, the AAP focused on the not-for-profit sector. On January 5, 1983, the *Chronicle of Higher Education* published and article about an AAP suit in the New York district court against New York University, nine faculty members, and a photocopy shop near the university. New York University settled out of court, agreeing to follow the 1976 guidelines and agreeing that faculty members who did not do so would not receive legal assistance from the institution if they were named as parties in a future copyright infringement suit. At about the same time, a Los Angeles secondary school teacher lost an infringement suit on the same grounds, namely, failure to follow the 1976 guidelines. In 1984, the National Music Publishers Association persuaded the University of Texas at Austin to stop allegedly illegal photocopying of music by its music department.

Though it is true copyright holders do have rights, the law clearly states that libraries and other users do too. As Scott Bennett wrote:

> We should respect the copyright law. This means understanding the law so that we can obey it an benefit from it. It means a refusal to wink at violations of the law, however widespread, just as it means advancing no untenable claims either to copyright protection or to fair use. Most important, it means acknowledging there are many genuinely debatable issues before us that will need to be resolved through negotiation, legislation, and litigation. Respecting the copyright law means making judicious use of these methods of resolving differences.
>
> We should keep the Constitutional purposes of copyright in view; honour those purposes; and work to give them vitality.

Without question, the most contentious issue is the electronic environment and who owns what, where, and how. The professional literature is full of articles exploring this or that aspect of the problem. Certainly, licensing of information, be it a CD-ROM, an online service, or an electronic journal, is at issue. Sometimes changes in the law assist in library operations, such as the amendment that authorizes libraries to make backup copies of computer programs

Then one reads articles asking: "Will electronic journals fulfill the current role of assessment that print-on-paper does?" and "How are electronic journal publishers to make money out of document delivery?" These articles leave one wondering how the voice of the user can be heard. One speculates whether librarians ever read licensing agreements, much less ask the institution's legal counsel to review such documents. Some agreements come in wrapped packages, so that one cannot read the full text until after one has opened the package, but the package carries words to the effect that "opening this package constitutes acceptance of the licensing agreement." A particularly good article discussing these issues is Laura Gasaway's "Copyright in the Electronic Era." Both "shrinkwrap" and "click-warp" licenses have been deemed legal by the courts.

Contractual Compliance

Following the various guidelines is one obvious way to achieve a limited form of compliance. (To date, there have been no suits in which the defendants claimed that they followed the guidelines; however, that does not mean there will not be such a suit.) For some libraries, the guidelines are too narrow and the cost of acquiring, processing, and housing the needed copyrighted material is high. Are these libraries and information centers cut off from needed information? Not if they have enough money.

The Copyright Clearance Center (CCC) is a not-for-profit service designed to serve libraries and other users of copyrighted material by providing system; CCC does not copy documents, but functions as a clearing house. Several thousand organizations are members; many, if not most, of these are libraries and information services. The CCC handles both U.S. and foreign publications.

The fees can be substantial when one realizes that the charge is for one article; however, the cost of a lawsuit would be higher, and if the organization lost, it could be forced to pay as much as $50,000 plus other costs and fees.

When in doubt, ask for permission. The process can be complicated when one must go directly to the copyright owner, but that is often the only option. Libraries can help make it easier in various ways. Tom Steele reported on a project at Wake Forest University that has helped make the process easier, if not painless. Two library staff members designed a Website with a list of publishers, a list of journals, a set of form letters for permission requests. and links to sites that provide information about copyright.

Licensing Agreements

Licensing is another method to achieve compliance. The CCC offers an annual license for publications it handles. Robert Oakely suggested a potentially useful approach to some of the copyright and preservation concerns in terms of journals. His suggestion was based on the idea that many, if not most, publishers do not have significant backfiles in a digital format. (Perhaps one could go further and suggest that they do not want to commit too many resources to maintaining very-low-revenue material in either print or digital formats.) According to Oakely, this situation presents an opportunity for joint ventures between libraries and publishers. Libraries engage in what they have always done, preserve information, and publishers produce it, In return, libraries would receive access to the backfile materials. Such arrangements would probably be through a contact or license.

What is the relationship between copyright and licenses? Perhaps the best short description of the similarities and differences was written by Ann Oakerson:

- Copyright represents a set of general regulations negotiated through statutory enactment. The same laws guidelines apply to everyone in the country.
- Licenses are contracts.. [that] represent [a] market-driven approach to such regulation. Each license is arranged between a willing surveyor and willing licensee, resource by resource. The owner of a piece of property is free to ask whatever price and set whatever conditions the market will bear.

More and more producers and libraries are turning to contracts or licenses to handle access and use.

Typical licensing agreements outline the lessee's responsibility for such things as security, customer service, payment and delivery, limitations and warranties, termination, indemnification, and assignment. All of these factors can affect the expected use. Though having to and attorney fees to the cost of building a collection is unappealing, the fact is that most of the producers will negotiate changes, and librarians should demand changes that benefit or at least do not create unreasonable demands on libraries and customers.

The library should maintain a master file of copies of all the licensing agreements and contracts. There should be a contact person who is responsible for knowing the terms of these documents as well as for being able to answer or secure answers to questions about the agreements. Compliance is a key issue, and the library or information center must do what it can to ensure compliance. However, some licensing agreements contain language that places responsibility on the library (subscriber) to monitor what users do with material after they leave the premises. Such clauses are beyond any library's or information center's ability to handle, and librarians should insist that they be deleted from the agreement.

The key is knowing what is in the agreement before purchasing. As with computer software, the licensing agreement often comes with the product that is, after the purchase. It is sealed in a package with a warning message to the effect that opening the package constitutes accepting the terms of the agreement inside the package. When considering a product from a new vendor, ask for a copy of the licensing agreement before making a final decision to purchase. This gives the staff an opportunity to review the document. It also provides an opportunity to request changes that the vendor may or may not be willing to make. In any event, it will give the library a chance to consider whether it can live with the conditions of the licensing agreement before committing to the purchase.

Because licensing is becoming a major and ever-growing issue for libraries, we include the "Principles" for licensing electronic resources as proposed by a number of library associations in North America in 1997.

Principles

1. A license agreement should state clearly what access

rights are being acquired by the licensee-permanent use of the content or access rights only for a defined period of time.

2. A license agreement should recognize and not restrict or abrogate the rights of the licensee or its user community permitted under copyright law. The licensee should make clear to the licensor those uses critical to its particular users including, but not limited to, printing, down loading, and copying.
3. A license agreement should recognize the intellectual property rights of both the licensee and the licensor.
4. A license agreement should not hold the licensee liable for unauthorized uses of the licensed resource by its users, as long as the licensee has implemented reasonable and appropriate methods to notify its user community of use restrictions.
5. The licensee should be willing to undertake reasonable and appropriate methods to enforce the terms of access to a licensed resource.
6. A license agreement should fairly recognize those access enforcement obligations which the licensee is able to implement without unreasonable burden. Enforcement must not violate the privacy and confidentiality of authorized users.
7. The licensee should be responsible for establishing policies that create an environment in which authorized users make appropriate use of licensed resources and for carrying out due process when it appears that use may violate the agreement.
8. A license agreement should require the licenser to give the licensee notice of any suspected or alleged

license violations that come to the attention of the licenser and allow a reasonable time for the licensee to investigate and take corrective action, if appropriate.

9. A license agreement should not require the use of an authentication system that is a barrier to access by authorized users.

10. When permanent use of a resource has been licensed, a license agreement should allow the licensee to copy data for the purposes of preservation and/or the creation of a usable archival copy. If a license agreement does not permit the licensee to make a usable preservation copy, a license agreement should specify who has permanent archival responsibility for the resource and under what conditions the licensee may access or refer users to the archival copy.

11. The terms of a license should be considered fixed at the time the license is signed by both parties. If the terms are subject to change (for example, scope of coverage or method of access), the agreement should require the licenser or licensee to notify the other party in a timely and reasonable fashion of any such changes before they are implemented, and permit either party to terminate the agreement if the changes are not acceptable.

12. A license agreement should require the licenser to defend, indemnify, and hold the licensee harmless from any action based on a claim that use of the resource in accordance with the license infringes any patent, copyright, trade-mark, or trade secret of any third party.

13. The routine collection of use data by either party to license agreement should be predicated upon disclosure of such collection activities to the other party and must respect laws and institutional policies regarding confidentiality and privacy.
14. A license agreement should not require the licensee to adhere to unspecified terms in a separate agreement between the licenser and a third party unless the terms are fully reiterated in the current license or fully disclosed and agreed to by the licensee.
15. A license agreement should provide termination rights that are appropriate to each party.

Summing Up

Copyright assures persons or organizations the right to seek tangible rewards from the production of creative or informative works. Without users of copyrighted materials, the producers would realize little or nothing from their efforts. Producers and users need to work together or everyone will lose. It would be desirable if once again we became partners in the dissemination of information and knowledge, rather than antagonists. Whatever does develop will not change the fact that it will not be possible to develop a library collection without considering the impact of copyright laws. Librarians should work to maintain a fair balance, but they must work primarily for the users because users have few spokespersons.

It is worth mentioning here that Digital library projects are moving ahead in many libraries and much has been said about the benefits of being able to access information once it is in digital form. Because of copyright restriction, there are limitations on what can be digitized... What will happen when [we] look to digitize material[s] of greater mainstream interest that are under copyright? What kinds of charges will be suggested by copyright holders? Can libraries afford them?

Glossary

Abstracts - Summaries, usually of journal articles. Searchable collections of references with abstracts are known as bibliographic databases. The term 'Abstracts' is sometimes used to refer to printed indexes of publications which include an abstract for each item listed.

ACQ STAFF - Used in Library Catalogue records to indicate that this is a new item which has recently arrived in the library and will be available soon.

Athens - An authentication system allowing you to access a large number of electronic resources, both on and off campus.

Bath - Used on UWE Library Services web pages to indicate the Bath Campus of UWE, which is at the Royal United Hospital (RUH) Bath. The Academy Library, RUH, Bath is an NHS-run Library that UWE Health and Social Care staff and students are entitled to join. Not to be confused with the University of Bath.

Bibliographic databases - Indexes to the contents of journals and other publications covering particular subject areas. Bibliographic databases are intended as finding tools, and do not provide full text, but give bibliographic references and usually include abstracts. The items listed are not necessarily available in the library or in electronic format.

Bibliographic references - Descriptions of whole publications (e.g. books) or parts of publications (e.g. journal articles) in a standard format. A bibliographic reference contains sufficient information to enable a potential user to identify and locate the item, and includes the author(s) and title, and details of when, where and by whom it was published.

BIDS - Bath Information and Data Services: a JISC national datacentre providing access to various electronic resources.

Boolean operators - Boolean Logic uses the operators AND, OR and NOT to link keywords and phrases in order to perform precise searches.

CHEST - The Combined Higher Education Software Team, part of Eduserv, which negotiates and manages agreements and licences for commercial electronic resources within UK education.

Commitment statement - A declaration by an organization of its intention to retain and make available a given object or set of objects. This may include such things as the length of time an object identifier will be valid and how invariant the object's content will be.

Complex digital object - Includes two or more content files (and their format variants or derivatives) and corresponding metadata. The content files are related as parts of a whole and are sequenced logically, such as pages. For example, a complex digital object could consist of a multi-page diary scanned as TIFF images, from which are generated display images (JPEGs and GIFs), plus a transcription of the diary and the metadata for each file. See also digital object, simple digital object.

Conference papers - Individual papers, similar to journal articles, usually published in a volume of conference proceedings. Individual conference papers are not included in the Library Catalogue.

Conference proceedings - A collection of conference papers presented at a particular conference, often published in book format, and sometimes as a special issue of a journal. Conference proceedings held in the library are listed in the Library Catalogue.

CrossRef - A collaborative reference linking service. See the CrossRef web site for more information.

Databases - Collections of organised searchable information. In a library context the term is generally used to refer to bibliographic databases, but can also refer to full text databases and collections of data (e.g. statistics).

Dim archive - An archive that is inaccessible to the public, but that can easily be made accessible if required. It's typically used for the preservation of content that is accessible elsewhere. See also dark archive, light archive.

Drop-down menu - A selection field that only displays one choice at first; the list box is hidden until the user expands it by clicking on it with the mouse or some other action. It is not the same thing as a pull-down menu.

Education resources collection - A collection of resources to support students in the Faculty of Education, situated on Level 5 of the Frenchay Campus (Bolland) Library.

Electronic journals - Journals published in electronic format. All the individual electronic journals available at UWE are listed on the Library Catalogue. Collections of electronic journals from a single publisher or supplier are listed in the library's list of electronic resources.

ERC - Used as a prefix to the Shelf Mark in Library Catalogue records to indicate items held in the Education Resources Collection situated on Level 5 of the Frenchay Campus (Bolland) Library.

Faculty librarians - Librarians who have responsibility for the library resources and information services relating to particular faculties. They are responsible for liaison between the library and relevant faculty and training and assisting users to make the best use of library resources.

Full-text databases - Electronic resources containing the full text of all or most items, often journal articles, rather than just abstracts.

Full-text harvest - The harvest of text from target pages to build a full-text index with links to the target resources. This is the same thing Google and other search engines do when performing a search.

Holds - Reservations placed on books that are on loan. You can place a hold using the Library Catalogue. Holds can only be placed on items that are on loan, or on the shelf at a campus other than your home campus.

Home campus - The campus where your faculty is based. If your faculty is based on more than one campus, it is the campus where you spend the majority of your time.

In transit - Used in Library Catalogue records to indicate that the item is in the process of being transferred from one campus library to another, in connection with inter-campus loans.

Inter-campus loans - Transfer of books held at one UWE campus library so that you can collect them from another campus library, usually your home campus library.

Inter-campus photocopies - Photocopy requests for items (usually journal articles) held at one UWE campus library that can be collected from another campus library, usually your home campus library.

Inter-library loans - Loan and photocopy requests for items not held in UWE libraries. Items held at other UWE campus libraries should be requested as inter-campus loans or inter-campus photocopies.

Inventory definition - A document signed by both the producer and Digital Preservation Repository staff that describes an inventory and records the negotiated data model, profile, rights agreements, and transmission method.

ISBN - International Standard Book Number. Every published book title has a unique ISBN. Different editions of the same book, and hardback and paperback versions of the same edition, have unique ISBNs. ISBNs appear in Library Catalogue records.

JISC - The Joint Information Systems Committee: supports the use if IT in UK further and higher education. Negotiates and manages agreements and licences for commercial electronic resources.

Journal articles - Individual articles, often on very specific topics, published in journals. Journal articles are not listed in the Library Catalogue (apart from single articles which have been photocopied and are available on Short Loan). You can search for journal articles on particular topics using bibliographic databases and full-text databases.

Journals - Publications issued at regular intervals. Each issue contains several different journal articles. Many journals are now published as electronic journals. All journal titles available, regardless of format, are listed in the Library Catalogue.

Keywords - Words and phrases that indicate the subject content of items listed in the Library Catalogue, bibliographic databases and full-text databases .

Librarians - To the layperson a librarian is anyone who works in a library, but the designation 'librarian' refers to those members of library staff who have a professional qualification in librarianship. Most librarians are chartered members of CILIP (the Chartered Institute of Librarians and Information Professionals). The other main group of staff who work in the library are library assistants.

Library catalogue - The library catalogue lists the library's resources: books, journals and audiovisual items, in both print and electronic formats. Using your UWE ID number and Library PIN, you can place holds, renew books and check what books you have on loan and when they are due back.

Library PIN - A 4-digit number. Together with your UWE ID number, it can be used to place holds, renew books, check what books you have on loan and when they are due back using the Library Catalogue, and borrow books using self-issue machines at some campus libraries. You also need your UWE ID number and Library PIN to access the Digital Collections.

Light archive - An archive that is accessible to the public. See also dim archive and dark archive.

MIMAS - Manchester InforMation and Associated Services: a JISC national datacentre providing access to various electronic resources.

Missing - Used in Library Catalogue records to indicate that a copy of the item is missing.

NISW-Store - Used in Library Catalogue records to indicate that the item is held in the archive collection of the National Institute for Social Work (now the Social Care Institute for Excellence). This collection is held in the UWE Store on the Frenchay Campus and books can be requested (for collection at any campus library) by placing a hold on each item required.

Object identifier - The primary identifier for a digital object within the Digital Preservation Repository, usually an ARK.

OpenURL - An academic unit established by UC to provide a supportive infrastructure for interdisciplinary research complementary to the academic goals of departments of instruction and research.

Periodicals - Periodicals are also known as journals, which is the term used in UWE libraries.

Portal - A web site or service that provides access to online resources, such as digital objects.

Pre-submission - A one-time process of information gathering and negotiation between the producer and Digital Preservation Repository staff regarding the possible ingest of a set of objects. This process usually culminates in the signing of a submission agreement and an inventory definition.

Reference - Used in Library Catalogue records to indicate that the item cannot be borrowed. Reference indicates the loan type of an item, and not its location, which is indicated by its Shelf Mark.

Reference area - An area in the library containing dictionaries, encyclopedias, directories etc. If an item is in the Reference Area, this is indicated as a prefix to the Shelf Mark in the Library Catalogue.

Schema - A common way of defining the structure, elements, and attributes that are available for use in a XML document that complies to the schema.

SCIE - Used in Library Catalogue records to indicate that the item has been supplied by SCIE (the Social Care Institute for Excellence)

SCONUL research extra - A scheme to enable academic staff and research students to borrow from many universities in the UK, administered by SCONUL.

Security backup - A second copy of a set of digital assets made to protect against loss due to unintended destruction or corruption of the primary set of digital assets. Security backups are created routinely and are not to be considered archives.

SFX - The link server from Ex Libris that allows context-sensitive linking between web resources in the scholarly information environment. SFX accepts an OpenURL as input from an information resource, which is referred to as an SFX source. See the SFX web page for more information.

Shelf mark - Used in Library Catalogue records to indicate the location where a book is shelved. For books this usually consists of a Dewey Decimal Classification number followed by the first three letters of the author's surname. Some Shelf Marks include a prefix (e.g. Reference Area) indicating that the book is shelved in a separate sequence.

Short loan - Used in Library Catalogue records to indicate Short Loan books, which can be borrowed for 4 hours or overnight, or over the weekend. Short loan books are kept in a separate Short Loan area at each campus library.

Smart crawl - A focused crawl based on dynamic criteria. For example, a crawler could be programmed to analyze and evaluate a web site for volatility, the presence of metadata, or the structure and content of a site, etc. The more it crawls, the smarter it gets about what to crawl and what not to crawl.

Stack - A closed-access area in the Frenchay Campus (Bolland) Library. Items from the Stack can be requested from the Frenchay Campus (Bolland) Library Enquiry Desk.

Standard access - A general access path provided by the CDL and the OAC, namely the OAC database. Customized access or portal to the depositor's digital assets is the responsibility of the depositor and not the CDL or the OAC.

Structural metadata - Metadata used to indicate the logical or physical relationship of the content files comprising the complex digital object, e.g., the sequence of pages for a group of images of a diary or of detailed images of a larger image. The structural metadata specifies a coherent presentation of the digital content and its pertinent associated metadata.

Subject gateways - Catalogues of key Internet resources in particular subject areas. Resources are selected and evaluated by subject specialists. Subject gateways can be used instead of search engines to identify fewer, but higher quality resources.

Submission agreement - A legal document through which the producer grants the Digital Preservation Repository the right to electronically store, convert, and copy digital assets for preservation purposes.

Submit - The act of transmitting a prepared digital object for deposit into the Digital Preservation Repository. Objects are prepared in accordance with the submission agreementand the CDL Guidelines for Digital Objects.

Submitter - A person or client system authorized by the producer to submit objects to the Digital Preservation

Repository. A submitter also has the rights of a consumer.

Surface - Includes materials that are publicly available by HTTP, are easily discoverable by crawlers, and are indexed by public indexes such as Google. Sometimes referred to as the static web. The opposite of the deep web.

Tag - A short, formal name used to indicate data structure or metadata elements, such as (title) in HTML or (unittitle) in EAD.

Targeted crawl - A web limited to particular web sites based on desired content (compare to a focused crawl. A targeted crawl may or may not be customized.

UWE store - Used in Library Catalogue records to indicate that the book or journal is held in a closed-access store on the Frenchay Campus, where older books and journals are located. Books from the UWE Store can be requested by placing a hold on each item. Journals can be requested at the Frenchay Campus (Bolland) Library Enquiry Desk, or photocopies of journal articles can be requested from other campuses as inter-campus photocopies.

Workroom - Used in Library Catalogue records to indicate that the item has been removed from the shelves, usually because it is in need of repair. If the item can be repaired it will be returned to the shelves. If it is beyond repair, it will either be replaced or withdrawn from stock.

Bibliography

Acuff, R., L. Fagan, T. Rindfleisch, B. Levitt, and P. Ford. Lightweight, mobile e-mail for intra-clinic communication. In *Proceedings of the 1997 AMIA Annual Fall Symposium*, pages 729-33, Oct 1997.

Aggarwal, N., *Digital Cataloguing and Classificaiton,* Rajat, New Delhi, 2006.

Aitchison, Jenny. “Library Services for Postgraduate Distance Education Students: Some Issues Examined in the Literature.” *Innovation*, no. 18 (June 1999): 20-28.

Anderson, “Budgeting for Reference Services in an Online Age.

Anita S. Harbert and Leon H. Ginsberg, *Human Services for Older Adults: Concepts and Skills,* 2nd revised (Columbia, SC: University of South Carolina Press, 1990): 3,54-80.

Anthony M. Cummings, *University Libraries and Scholarly Communica-tion: A Study Prepared for the Andrew W. Mellon Foundation,* (Washington, D.C.: The Association of Research Libraries for The Andrew W. Mellon Foundation, 1992), pp. xvi-xviii.

ARL Statistics, 1992-93, (Washington, D.C.: Association of Research Libraries, 1994), “*Total Operating Expenditures*.”

Barbara T. Mates, *Library Technology for Visually and Physically Impaired Patrons,* (Westport: Meckler, 1991).

Beagle, Donald. "Web-based Learning Environments: Do Libraries Matter?" *College & Research Libraries* 61, no. 4 (July 2000): 367-379.

Berry, Parasuraman, and Zeithaml, "Improving Service Quality in America," 32-52.

Betty J. Turock, "Public Library Service for Older Adults: Update 1984, "*Library Quarterly* 57 (April 1987): 143.

Betty J. Turock, *Information and Aging* (Jefferson, NC.: McFarland, 1988).

Betty J. Turock, *Serving the Older Adult: a Guide to Library Programmes and Information Sources* (New York: Bowker, 1982); Genevieve M. Casey, *Library Services for the Aging* (Hamden, CT: Library Professional Publications, 1984).

Bhagwal Das, *Successful Glossary of Common Library Terms,* Cyber Tech, New Delhi, 2009.

Bitner, Booms, and Tetreault, *The Service Encounter*.

Black, J.B., et. al., *Surveying Public Libraries for the* ADA. (Pinellas County, Florida: Pinellas Public Library Cooperative, 1992).

Bowen and Lawler, "Total Quality-Oriented Human Resources Management," 29-41.

Braunstein, "Costs and Benefits of Library Information," p. 81.

Burmanb, J.S., *Libraries and Reference Services,* Rajat, New Delhi, 2007.

Charles A. Bunge and Marjorie E. Murfin, "Reference Questions- Data from the Field, "*RQ* 27 (1987): 15-18.

Christopher G. Lewis, "The Americans with Disabilities Act and its Effect on Public Libraries, "*Public Libraries 31* (January/February 1992): 23-8.

Christopher W. Nolan, "Closing the Reference Interview: Implications for Policy and Practice, " RQ 31 (Summer 1992): 513-523.

Clay Carr, "Total Quality Training," *Training* 27 (November 1990): 59-65.

Connie Van Fleet, "Lifelong Learning Theory and the Provision of Adult Services" *in Adult Services: an Enduring Focus for Public Libraries,* ed. Kathleen M. Heim and Danny P. Wallace (Chicago: ALA, 1990), pp. 166-265.

Craven, Jenny and Peter Brophy. "Lifelong Learning and Libraries: An Annotated Bibliography." *New Review of Libraries and Lifelong Learning* 1 (2000): 155-172.

Cropley, A.J., *Lifelong Education: a Psychological Analysis* (New York: Pergamon, 1977), pp. 57-58, Wills W. Harman, "Recent Psychological and Psychic Research: Implications for Science and Society," *in The Future of Education: Policy Issues and Challenge,* ed. Kathryn Cirincione-Coles (Beverly Hills: Sage, 1981), p. 218.

Darlene E. Weingand, "The Invisible Client: Meeting the Needs of Persons With Learning Disabilities," *The Reference Librarian 31* (1990): 77-88.

David E. Bowen and Edward E. Lawler III, "Total Quality-Oriented Human Resources Management, "*Organizational Dynamics* 20 (Spring 1992):29-41.

Denise Perry Donavin, *Aging with Style and Savvy* (Chcago: ALA, 1990), p. 27, reporting on *Love, Sex, and Aging: a Consumers Union Report,* Edward M. Brecher and the Editors of Consumer Reports Books (PLACE, Little, Brown, 1984).

Digest of Education Statistics, 1993, Table 403, p.427. The most recent, comprehensive data available.

Don Fersh and Peter W. Thomas, *Complying with the Americans with Disabilities Act: a Guidebook for Management and People with Disabilities* (Westport: Quorum Books, 1993).

Donald E. Peterson and John Hillkirk, *A Better Idea : Refining time Way Americans Work* (Boston: Houghton Mifflin, 1991).

Edward E. Lawler III, "Total Quality Management and Employee Involvement; Are They Compatible?" Academy of Management Executive 8 (1994): 68-76.

Elaine Landau, "The Challenge of Film Programming for Older Adults, "*The Bookmark* 42 (Winter 1984): 102.

Elinor B. Waters and Jane Goodman, Empowering *Older Adults: Practical Strategies for Counselors* (San Francisco: Jossey-Bass Publishers, 1990): p. xi.

Elizabeth Vierck, Fact Book on Aging (Santa Barbara, CA: ABC-CLIO, 1990): 3.

Francoise Hebert, "Service Quality: An Unobtrusive Investigation of Interlibrary Loan in Large Public Libraries in Canada," *Library & Information Studies Research* 16 (1994): 3-21.

Gibson, Andrew, Robert Newton, and David Dixon. "Supporting Open and Distance Learners: Practice and Policy Across Further and Higher Education Libraries." *Library Review* 48, no. 5 (1999): 219-231.

Gregory Lozier, G. and Deborah J. Teeter, "Six Foundations of Total Quality Management," *New Directions for Institutional Research* 78 (Summer 1993): 5-11.

Hudson, Elizabeth A., *Libraries for a Lifetime* (Oklahoma City: The Oklahoma Department of Libraries, 1989).

Ismail-Kaye, Nazira. "International Centre for Distance Learning (ICDL) and Services to Distance Learners." Paper presented at the *AAOU Pre-Conference Seminar on Outreach Library Services for Distance Learners,* February 20, 2002, New Delhi, India.

James E. Swiss, "Adapting Total Quality Management (TQM) to Government, "Public *Administration Review 52* (July/August 1992): 356-362.

Jan Mattson. "Improving Service Quality in Person-to-Person Encounters: Integrating Findings from a Multi-disciplinary Review," *The Services Industries Journal* 14 (January 1994): 45-61.

Janet Dagnenais Brown, "Using Quality Concepts to Improve Reference Services," *College & Research Libraries* (May 1994): 211-219.

Joanne L. Crispin, ed., *The Americans with Disabilities Act. Its Impact on Libraries The Library's Responses in "Doable" Steps,* (Chicago: American Library Association, 1993).

John J. Jax and Theresa Muraski, "Library Services for Students with Disabilities at the University of Wisconsin-Stout, "*The Journal of Academic Librarianship* 19 (July 1993): 166-68.

John Pulse, "Customer Focus: The Salvation of Service Organizations," *Public Library Journal* 6 (1991): *1-5.*

Joyce G. Saricks and Nancy Brown, *Reader's Advisory Service in the Public Library* (Chicago: ALA, 1989).

Jurow, "Tools for Measuring and Improving Performance," 113-126.

Keith C. Wright and Judith F. Davie, *Serving the Disabled* (New York: Neal-Schuman Publishers, 1991).

Kordupleski, Rust, and Zahorik, "Why Improving Quality Doesn't Improve Quality," 82-95.

Lancaster, F.W., *If you want to evaluate your library...* , 2nd ed., (Cham-paign, Illinois: Graduate School of Library and Information Science, University of Illinois, 1993), p. 159.

Lawler, "Total Quality Management and Employee Involvement, " 68-76.

Leonard L Berry, A. Parasuraman, and Valerie A Zeithaml, "The Service Quality Puzzle," *Business Horizons* (September-October 1988): 35-43.

Leonard L. Berry, A. Parasuraman, and Valerie A. Zeithmal, "Improving Service in Quality America: Lessons

Learned, "Academy of Management Executive 8 (1994): 32-52.

Library Trends 41 (Summer 1992) Libraries Serving an Underserved Population: Deaf and Hearing-Impaired Patrons.

Lowrence O. Gostin and Henry A. Beyer, eds., *Implementing the Americans with Disabilities Act: Rights and Responsibilities of all Americans* (Baltimore: P. H. Brookes Pub. Co., 1993).

Lozier and Teeter. "Six Foundations of Total Quality Management," *5-11*.

Lydia Olzak, "Mistakes and Failures at the Reference Desk," *RQ* 31 (Fall 1991): 39-49.

Mairead Browne and Susan Edwards. "How Users Assess the Quality of an Information Service," in Peter Clayton and Russell McCaskie, eds., *Priorities for the Future* (Deakin, Australia: Australian Library and Information Associa-tion, 1992).

Mark S. Ackerman. Providing social interaction in the digital library. In *Proceedings of the First Annual Conference on the Theory and Practice of Digital Libraries*, 1994.

Markland, Margaret. "The Integration of Digital Libraries and Online Information Resources into the Online Learning Environment: An Annotated Bibliography and Discussion." *New Review of Libraries and Lifelong Learning* 3 (2002): 3-15.

Martin Cummings, *The Economics of Research Libraries*, (Washington, D.C.: Council on Library Resources, Inc., 1986), p. 7.

Martin cummings, *The Economics of Research Libraries,* p. 77.

Mary Jo Brazil, *Building Library Collections on Aging: a Selection Guide and Core List* (Santa Barbara, CA: ABC-CLIO,1990).

Mattson, "Improving Service Quality in Person-to-Person Encounters," 45-61; J. Joseph Cronin, J. and Steven A. Taylor, "SERVPERF Versus SERVQUAL: Reconciling Performance-Based and Perceptions-Minus-Expecta-tions Measurement of Service Quality." *Journal of Marketing 58* (January 1994): 125-131.

Melanie J. Norton, "Effective Bibliographic Instruction for Deaf and Hearing-Impaired College Students, "*Library Trends 41 (*Summer 1992): 118-50.

Michael G. Gunde, "Libraries and the Americans with Disabilities Act, " pp. 1-31 and Ruth O'Donnel, "Planning to Implement the ADA in the Library," pp. 32-70 in Donald D. Foos and Nancy C. Pack, eds., *How Libraries Must Comply with the Americans with Disabilities Act.* (ADA) (Phoenix: Oryx Press, 1992).

Miriam A. Drake and Harold A. Olsen, "The Economics of Library Innovation," *Library Trends* 28 (Summer 1979): 102.

Muffin, "Cost Analysis of Library Reference Services," pp. 1-14. See also, Anderson, "Budgeting for Reference Services in an Online Age," pp. 185-186.

Nancy A. Can House and Thomas A. Childers, "The use of Public Library Roles for Effectiveness, "*Library & Information Science Research* 16 (1994): 41-58.

Nancy A. Van House, Beth T. Weil. and Charles R. McClure, *Academic Library Performance: A Practical Approach* (Chicago: American Library Associa-tion. 1990).

Newlin, B. "Traveling the New Information Superhighway". *Small Press* 12 (Spring 1994): 26-29.

One Book Five Ways. Los Altos, Calif.: William Kaufmann, 1977.

Parasuraman, A., Valerie A. Zeithaml, and Leonard L. Berry, "Reassessment of Expectations as a Comparison Standard in Measuring Service Quality: Implications for Further Research." *Journal of Marketing 58* (January 1994): 111- 124.

Patrick Penland, "Adult Self-Planned Learning," *Public Libraries* 17 (Summer 1978): 6-8; Allen Tough, *The Adults Learning Projects: a Fresh Approach to Theory and Practice in Adult Learning, 2nd ed.* (Austin, TX: Learning Concepts, 1979); Malcolm S. Knowles, *The Modern Practice of Adult Education,* revised and updated (Chicago: Association Press, 1980).

Paul B. Kantor, "Cost and Productivity in Library Operations," in *Pro-ductivity in the Information Age. Proceedings of the 46th ASIS Annual Meeting,* vol. 20, (Washington, D.C.: American Society for Information Science, 1983), p. 298.

Paul S. Adler and Terry Winograd, editors. *Usability : turning technologies into tools.* Oxford University Press, 1992.

Paul, W., Vogt, *Dictionary of Statistics and Methodology: A Nontechnical Guide for the Social Sciences,* (Newbury Park: Sage Publications, 1993), p. 160.

Paula Brown Doress and Diana Laskin Siegal, *Ourselves, Growing Older: Women Aging with Knowledge and Power* (New York: Touchstone, 1987).

Peter T. Ewell, "Assessment and TQM: In Search of Convergence," *New Directions for Institutional Research* 71 (Fall 1991): 39-52.

Phyllis Dalton, "Exemplary Library Programmes and Services for Those with Disabilities," 27-33 in Joanne L. Crispin, *The American with Disabilities Act.*

Posel, N. R. "High Priced or Over-Priced They're Every Library's Problem". *Reference Librarian* 19 (1987): 257-67.

Rao Aluri, "Improving Reference Service: The Case for Using a Continu-ous Quality Improvement Method," *RQ* 33 (Winter 1993): 220-236.

Raymond E. Kordupleski, Roland T. Rust, and Anthony J. Zahorik, "Why Improving Quality Doesn't Improve Quality or Whatever Happened to Market-ing?" *California Management Review 35* (Spring 1993): 82-95.

Reka Albert, Albert-Laszlo Barabasi, and Hawoong Jeong. Diameter of the World Wide Web. *Nature*, 401(6749), September 1999.

Rettig, J. "Do Publishers Have Ears?" *Wilson Library Bulletin* 62 (January 1988) 15-22.

Rhea J. Rubin and Gail McGovern, *Working with older Adults: A Handbook for Libraries, 2nd* (Sacaramento, CA: California State Library, 1988).

Richard M. Hodgetts, Fred Luthans, and Sang M. Lee, "New Paradigm Organizations: From Total Quality to Learning World Class, "*Organizational Dynamics* 22 (Winter 1994): 5-19.

Robert B. Allen and Jane Acheson. Browsing the structure of multimedia stories. In *Proceedings of the Fifth ACM International Conference on Digital Libraries*, 2000.

Robert B. Allen. A multi-timeline interface for historical newspapers. In *Proceedings of the Fifth ACM / IEEE-CS Joint Conference on Digital Libraries*, 2005.

Roby Kidd, J., *How Adults Learn* (New York: Association Press, 1959), p. 90; K. A. McClelland, "Self-conception and Life Satisfaction: Integrating Aged Subculture and Activity Theory, "*Journal of Gerontoglogy* 37 (1982): 723.

Salace, J. "Video Distribution: The Maze Made Manageable". *Library Journal* 115 (July 1990): 42-44.

Sexton, M. "Replacing the Myths About Marketing to Libraries". *Publishers Weekly* 236 (March 10, 1989): 56-57.

Shauglmessy, "Benchmarking, Total Quality Management, and Libraries," 7-12.

Slade, Alexander L. "Research on Library Services for Distance Learning: An International Perspective." *In Information Services in an Electronic Environment*, edited by G. E. Gorman. International Yearbook of Library and Information Management 2001/2002. London: Library Association Publishing, 2001, 187-233. Reprinted in *Journal of Library & Information Services in Distance Learning* 1, no. 1 (2004): 5-43.

Sloan, Bernie and Sharon Stoerger. Library Support for Distance Learning. November 2002.

Stewart, J. and M. Clarke, "The Public Service Orientation: Issues and Dilemmas, "*Public Administration* 65 (Summer 1987): 161-177.

Susan Jurow, "Tools for Measuring and Improving Performance," *Journal of Library Administration* 18 (1993): 113-126.

Swiss, "Adapting Total Quality Management (TQM) to Government," 356-362.

Thomas A. Myers, *An Analysis of Perceived Customer Contact Service Quality in the Public Sector* (D.P.A. dissertation. Virginia Commonwealth Uni-versity, School of Community and Public Affairs, 1990).

Thomas W. Shaughnessy, "Benchmarking, Total Quality Management' and Libraries." *Library Administration & Management* 7 (Winter 1993): 7-12.

Tim Burns, "Researching Customer Service in the Public Sector," *Journal of the Market Research Society* 34 (1992): *53-60.*

Tim Loney and Arnie Bellefontaine, "TQM Training: The Library Service Challenge, "*Journal of Library Administration* 18 (1993): 85-95.

Wendy S. Zabara ford and Christina Nathan Etienne, "Can I Help You? A Framework for Interdisciplinary Customer Service Encounters," *Management Communications Quarterly* 7 (May 1994): 413-441.

William Safire, *Safire's Political Dictionary,* (New York:

Random House, 1978), p. 808. The concept was popularized and expanded in Lester C. Thurow's *The Zero-Sum Society: Distribution and the Possibilities for Economic Change,* (New York: Basic Books, 1980).

Yale M. Braunstein, "Costs and Benefits of Library Information: The User Point of View," *Library Trends* 29 (Summer 1979): 80.

Index